LEAD FROM ANY SEAT

10 Ways to Get More Involved in Your Job, Make a Lasting Impact, and Advance Your Career - Fast!

ANDREI ANCA MBA, CLSSBB

Lead From Any Seat

ISBN: 9781791565732

Notice of Liability

Notice of Rights

Illustrations, design, and cover by Andrei Anca
Editing by Ken Ravitz
Proofing by Rebecca Rumbo
Some graphic elements by Zolee, www.onlygfx.com

Written and published by Andrei Anca
www.linkedin.com/in/andreianca
aanca@msn.com
www.LeadFromAnySeat.com

For all of you who hate mediocrity, are tired of being followers and are ready to lead and to make a positive impact on everything you touch.

ACKNOWLEDGMENTS

This book was a joy for me to write and design. I am happy to share what I have learned and observed during my career and I hope that this book will inspire others to take initiative and to make an impact on any job.

I want to thank Micky Nye for believing in me and introducing me to Lean Six Sigma, which helped me see everything through a continuous improvement lens.

I also want to thank my friend and Lean Six Sigma partner Ellen Guilfoyle for inspiring me with her go-getter attitude and her passion for performance excellence.

Thank you Maridel for gently pressuring me to finish this book by asking "So, how is the book?" every time we saw each other.

To Kenny, thank you for spending countless hours editing and proofing this book. And yes, now I know the difference between *from and form* and between *barley and barely*.

CONTENTS

"Remember to look up at the stars and not down at your feet. Try to make sense of what you see and wonder about what makes the universe exist. Be curious. And however difficult life may seem, there is always something you can do and succeed at. It matters that you don't just give up."

– Stephen Hawking

A DIFFERENT WAY OF THINKING

According to a Gallup study published in 2015, less than one-third of Americans are truly engaged in their job in any given year. This has been steady since the year 2000, when Gallup began measuring workplace engagement. They define engaged employees as those who are involved in their work, enthusiastic about coming to work, and committed to their work place. In other words, over two-thirds of employees don't really care much about their jobs.

I find it puzzling that most of us are indifferent about our jobs, and just go to work and sleepwalk through the workday. We just work for the paychecks. Furthermore, per the same study, employees' view of their managers accounts for at least 70% of the variance in employee engagement scores and one in two employees leave their job to get away from their manager. I have heard this before and I firmly believe it's true—people don't leave jobs, they don't leave companies; they leave their managers.

If we don't get along with our managers or if we don't like them and respect them, it is likely that we will leave a company, despite a high salary or competitive benefits. Few people actually enjoy changing jobs. It may be exciting in the beginning, but the honeymoon ends quickly. You get in a boring routine and all of a sudden you learn that the grass is not always greener—similar issues, different company. Well, now what? Wait a couple of years, get another job and this goes on and on. Chances are that you eventually get tired and frustrated and you have only two options: start your own business or keep changing jobs.

Starting a business is tempting and I do encourage you to follow your heart and your passion. Start a business, give it a try, and if you put in enough passion and hard work, your start-up could very well be among the 10% that succeed. I am not going to talk about what you need to do get started on your new business. There are so many books, blogs, videos, and courses on this topic. But I do have a word of advice: don't start a business just because you hate your boss and you want to be your own boss. That is not enough and it won't get you very far.

Now, even if starting a business is not for you or even if you are not a risk taker, you do have to pay your bills. In this case, you still have to go to work and work for a boss who, chances are, you do not like or respect. Perhaps after changing jobs many times, you do finally find a fairly bearable job and force yourself to tough it out and hang in there. But now you will face even bigger problems. Since you are so unhappy with your job, you probably bring all the frustrations home with you; all this mess will negatively impact your life in general. You and those around you will become miserable. If you spend one-third of your day doing something that you don't like and perhaps working for a manager that you hate, by the end of the day you are exhausted and can't wait for the weekend. What kind of existence is that?

Steve Jobs once said: "Your work is going to fill a large part of your life, and the only way to be truly satisfied is to do what you believe is great work. And the only way to do great work is to ***love*** what you do." Are you doing great work? Are you applying yourself one hundred percent? Are you making a difference?

BE A COFFEE BEAN

Yet another parable (author unknown) landed in my inbox recently, and I find it so meaningful that I thought it was worth including in this book. Even if you have heard it before, I encourage you to read it again.

The story goes like this:

A young woman went to her mother and told her about her life and how things were hard for her. She didn't know how she was going to make it and wanted to give up. She was tired of fighting and struggling. It seemed that when one problem was solved, a new one arose.

Her mother took her to the kitchen. She filled three pots with water and in the first pot she placed carrots, in the second one she placed eggs, and in the last pot she placed ground coffee beans.

She let them sit and boil without saying a word. In about twenty minutes, she turned off the burners. She took the carrots out of the water and she placed them in a bowl. She then pulled the eggs out and placed them in a bowl. Then, she ladled the coffee into a bowl. Turning to her daughter, she asked, "Tell me what you see?"

"Carrots, eggs, and coffee", she replied.

The mother brought her closer and asked her to feel the carrots. She did and she noted that they were soft. She then asked her to take an egg and break it. After peeling off the shell, she observed the hard-boiled egg. Finally, she asked her to sip the coffee. The daughter smiled, as she tasted its rich aroma.

The daughter then asked, "What's the point, mother?"

Her mother explained that each of these objects had faced the same adversity—boiling water— but each of them reacted differently. The carrot went in strong, hard, and unrelenting. After being subjected to the boiling water, however, it softened and became weak. The egg had been fragile. Its thin outer shell had protected its liquid interior. But, after being exposed to the boiling water, its inside became hardened. The ground coffee beans, however, were unique. After they were placed in the boiling water, they had changed the water.

"Which are you?" she asked the daughter. "When adversity knocks on your door, how do you respond? Are you a carrot, an egg, or a coffee bean?"

Now back to you. Are you the carrot that seems strong, but with pain and adversity, you wilt, become soft and lose your strength? Are you the egg that starts with a malleable heart, but changes with the heat? Or are you like the coffee bean that actually changes the hot water? When the water gets hot, it releases the fragrance and flavor. If you are like the coffee bean, when things are at their worst, you get better and change the situation around you.

While I am not a big fan of fables, this one really struck a chord with me. I realized that during my career so far, I have met mostly carrots and eggs and very few coffee beans. This is extremely disappointing—and it's not just because I dislike the taste of carrots and I love coffee. Why are people so afraid to initiate change, to make decisions, and to take risks? Why do people let themselves be influenced and controlled by the working environment—and all they do is complain? Do you notice that some people always pose as victims and how everything else is to blame because they never get promoted, because they have to work long hours while their co-workers always leave early, and the drama goes on and on? For them it is always someone else's fault and they are the *victim*.

NO MORE DRAMA

Back in the 1960s, psychotherapist Stephen Karpman created the Drama Triangle, a model of dysfunctional social interaction. Karpman observed that in conflict and drama, there is always "good guy vs. bad guy" thinking. He also observed that the participants become drawn in by the energy that the drama generates. The drama obscures the real issues, confusion escalates, and people are no longer focused on solutions. Each point of the triangle represents an ineffective response to conflict.

According to Karpman, people stuck in this triangle bounce around among three archetypal roles: Victim, Persecutor, and Rescuer, each one as unhelpful as the other.

Victims are hopeless and helpless. They are not actual victims; they just feel and act like victims. They have a "My life is so unfair; poor me" attitude and they blame others for what happens to them. It is never their fault. All they do is complain. They take no responsibility for fixing anything. The problem is that the victims feel like *change* is out of their control. They are just whiners, and nobody likes a whiner.

Persecutors usually blame the victims and criticize others and believe that they are surrounded by idiots who are inferior to them. They feel superior. They have a sense of power and control, but the problem is that they are the ones creating victims. They tend to be micro-managers because they don't trust anyone. They also have a hard time getting people to help them, because who likes a bully?

Rescuers are always working hard to "help" other people, mostly the victims. They often feel overwhelmed, because they feel like they have to constantly jump in to fix everything. Rescuers believe that they are indispensable, but people reject their help because nobody likes a meddler.

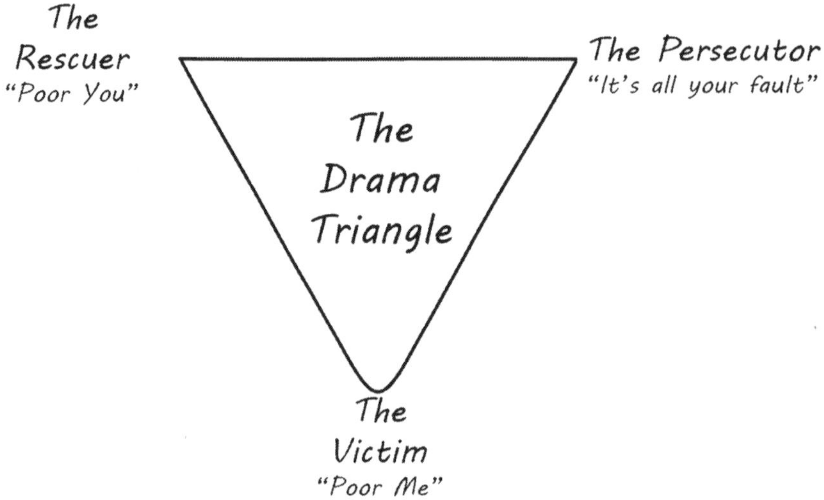

Figure 0.1 The drama triangle

Unfortunately, there are no winners in a Karpman Drama Triangle. Once you are in the triangle, all you get is drama. You have to escape as soon as possible, and the only way to do it is to stop participating as a victim, persecutor, or rescuer and move to the center. The center of the Drama Triangle combines elements from each corner: sensitivity, compassion, and responsibility. It is the optimal position for you to focus on solutions and to make a difference without alienating others.

Executive coach and author David Emerald created an alternative to the Drama Triangle, called The Empowerment Dynamic (TED). Emerald offers antidotes for each role and default behavior. He suggests replacing Victim with Creator, Persecutor with Challenger, and Rescuer with Coach. But creating and challenging means stepping out of our comfort zone and this could be risky. We are afraid to take risks because we are afraid of making mistakes and looking bad. We would rather do nothing, say nothing, and keep riding the wave of mediocrity. I strongly believe that any action is better than no action; you must take the challenge.

CHANGE IS SCARY

In my profession as a Change Leader, I encounter a lot of resistance because I bring change, and most people are scared of change. In every organization, however, there are a handful of people who would love to do things differently, but they are afraid to initiate anything because they don't know where to begin. If you are one of them, fear no more. After reading this book, I promise you that you will not only know what to do, but you will change your entire perspective about your job, your boss, and even your co-workers. You will see things differently since you will have a new tool box loaded with tools that will help you get organized and be as effective and as efficient as possible.

How to Use this Book

My goal is to persuade you that you have the opportunity to change everything you encounter at work—and in life in general—for the better. And you don't have to quit your current job. You just need to care, to get involved, and to change the way you approach your job.

"If you don't like something, change it. If you can't change it, change your attitude."

–Maya Angelou

In this book, you will find many process improvement tools that I have learned and used during my career in Lean Six Sigma and Business Process Management. Some of them are easy to understand, while others are more complex and require practice to master. I encourage you to take the time to understand each tool and to apply it to your own scenarios. You will see that some tools are universal and can be applied to many industries and even life situations, not just your job. The trick is to make sure that you have the patience to learn how and when to apply them and also to understand their value. I encourage you to explore each of them further. There is plenty of free information available on the Internet, but you must have the curiosity to learn more.

Once you understand and master these tools, you can use them individually or as part of a complete methodology. When I learned the tools, I applied them to Six Sigma projects as part of what is called the DMAIC methodology (Define, Measure, Analyze, Improve, and Control). Do not use any tool just for the sake of using it. They are meant to help you understand processes, eliminate waste, identify and implement improvements. Do not let any methodology, deliverables, or tools become the work.

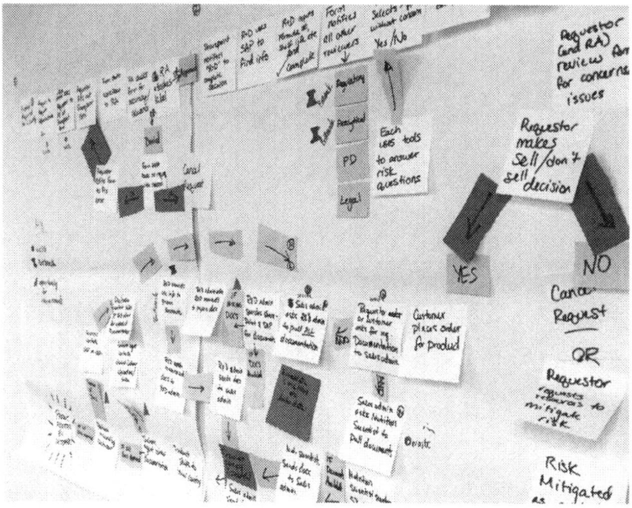

I typically apply most of the tools using Microsoft Visio and Excel, but if you don't have these programs or you don't know how to use them, don't worry. You can use any other similar products or even draw them by hand on a piece of paper. In fact, I prefer using a whiteboard or sticky notes on a wall, especially when using the tools during team meetings. This gets more interaction and participation from team members.

While these tools can help you add structure to your work, they will not help if you don't have the desire to drive change and to make a difference. Becoming a coffee bean is a prerequisite.

1. CHANGE YOUR PERSPECTIVE

"If you can't change the circumstances, change your perspective."

\- Unknown

YOUR BOSS IS YOUR CUSTOMER

The founder of Walmart, Sam Walton, once said: "There is only one boss. The customer. And he can fire everybody in the company from the chairman on down, simply by spending his money somewhere else." The customer of your company is indeed the biggest boss and the most powerful. Without customers, your company would not even exist. But this is the big picture. How does it translate to your level? While you may not interact with the external customers of your company, you definitely interact with your internal customers, and the biggest one in your case is none other than your boss. So, I challenge you from now on to change your perspective and think of your boss as your prime customer. Not only does your boss represent the company you work for, but the company that pays you to do a job is connected to you through your manager.

Think of your boss as your *paying* customer. You don't have to really like her to perform well. If you had your own business, what would you do if you didn't like your customers? Would you stop serving them? If you refuse to provide service, they will find someone else who can. Same with your employer. If your company—through your manager—is not happy with your services, what do you think will happen? They will let you go and find someone else.

As I mentioned in the introduction, chances are that if you leave your job, it's mostly because your manager drives you crazy or because you get frustrated or offended. I personally don't understand how people get offended so easily. I grew up in a Communist country where it was difficult finding food in the stores and satisfying basic survival needs. When we had so little, we didn't get offended easily. We just wanted the necessities: food, electricity, heat, and hot water. We had a totally different approach to life. But I understand, as circumstances change we must be assertive and stand up for ourselves. We don't have to tolerate and endure uncomfortable and frustrating situations anymore.

If you feel like you are not making enough of an impact—as I hear many millennials saying—you will probably start looking for another job right away. I am sad to see young employees come and go because they feel that they are not making an impact. When you ask them how long they have been with the company, the answer may be "almost seven months." First of all, seven months is not enough time for anybody to make an impact. Second, what have you done to make an impact with your number one customer—your boss? How did you serve your customer better than your competition—your peers and other employees?

In his book *Linchpin*, Seth Godin mentions how companies today are not looking for people who just do their job and follow directions. He believes that this outdated approach is the result of the brainwashing done by schools and by "the system." The rules worked for two hundred years, but not any longer. He is right on point. I agree with him not just because he is one of my favorite authors, but because I experience this every day at work. Following directions is not enough—at least not if you want to succeed and to make a difference.

The crucial first step in making an impact is to change the way you think about your boss. Think of your boss as your customer and not only will you start making an impact sooner, you will also be more appreciated and rewarded. All you have to do is to shift your focus from yourself to your customer.

As in any business, before you start serving your customers, you need to get to know your customers and understand their needs.

SEE THROUGH THE EYES OF YOUR CUSTOMER

Henry Ford said: "If there is one secret to success, it lies in the ability to get the other person's point of view and see things from that person's angle as well as from your own." This is such a simple statement, easy to understand and follow, yet the majority of us choose to ignore it.

More often than not, businesses are so passionate about their products or services that they forget that they must satisfy *customers'* needs, not their own. We, as employees, are guilty of making the same mistakes. We get so caught up in our daily routine, so eager to show our skill set and to impress, that we often neglect the needs of our manager, the needs of our stakeholders, and the needs of all our internal and external customers.

If you are committed to truly helping, you can't continue to put yourself first. It's not about you; it's about you serving others. If you hire a contractor to paint your living room, you are probably very specific about what you want. What if the contractor is also a mural painter who decides to paint a beautiful scene on your walls? What would you say? You may in fact like it, but that was not what you wanted. You may appreciate the talent of the painter, but you will be a dissatisfied customer. I am not saying you shouldn't be passionate and love the work you do, but I urge you to listen and understand what your customers really want.

"You can't just ask customers what they want and then try to give that to them," said Steve Jobs. "By the time you get it built, they'll want something new." What will they want next? To serve any customer over time, not only must you truly understand who they are, you also must learn as much as possible about them so you can anticipate their needs. While your main focus will be on internal customers, it's helpful to understand your external customers as well.

Before we even start talking about customers, do you understand what your company does? I find it alarming how many people know next to nothing about their company; they have no idea what industry it operates in, what products or services it offers, and whether it is a public or private company. You must have the curiosity to learn as much as possible about your company. Find out how and when the company was founded, what is its service/product offering, what markets it operates in, and how many sites it has. Does your company sell directly to consumers (BTC), to other businesses (BTB), or both? Who are they and what do they do? Why do they buy? What needs is your company trying to satisfy?

According to Maslow's Hierarchy of Needs, developed by the American psychologist Abraham Maslow, people are motivated to achieve certain needs. As soon as one need is fulfilled, they seek to satisfy the next one, and so on. Each lower-level need must be satisfied before a person can focus on the higher needs.

Maslow came up with five categories of needs after studying prominent figures such as Albert Einstein, Jane Addams, and Eleanor Roosevelt:

Physiological needs. Anything that the body needs in order to function properly and not fail: air, water, food, etc.

Safety needs. After people satisfy their physical needs, safety needs are next: personal and financial security, health and well-being.

Love and belonging. This is the third level of human needs. It is especially strong during childhood, when it can actually override the second need (the need for safety): friendship, family, and affection.

Esteem. People have the need to feel respected, to be valued and accepted by others. Maslow mentioned two different versions of esteem needs: lower and higher. The lower version of esteem is the need to be respected by others, including attention, fame, and status. The higher version of esteem is the need for self-respect. For example, people may have needs of strength, self-confidence and independence.

Self-actualization. This need refers to a person's full potential and the awareness of that potential. People may perceive this need differently. For example, one person may have the strong desire to form a large family. For other people, it may be expressed in paintings, pictures, or music.

With theses in mind, can you easily determine what needs your business satisfies?

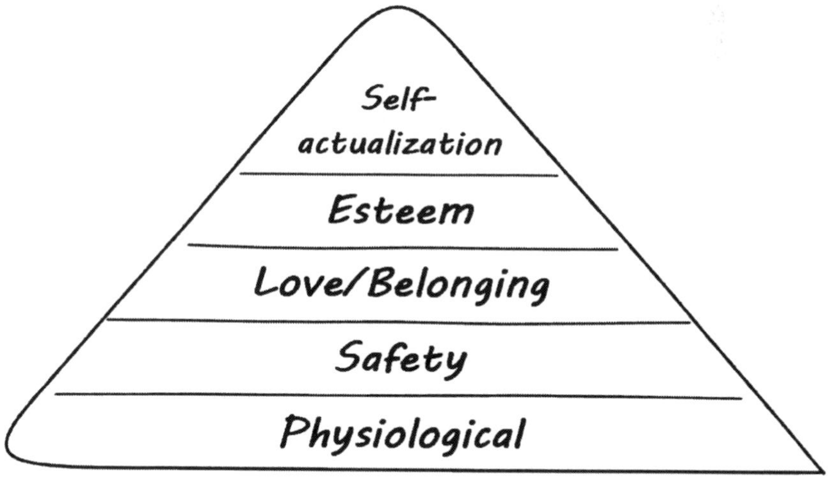

Figure 1.1: Maslow's Hierarchy of Needs Triangle

You are probably wondering why you need to know all these business details, especially if you don't have any direct contact with customers. Unless you work in Sales, Marketing, or Customer Service, chances are you have minimal or no interaction with the final customers. The answer is simple: understanding as much as possible about your employer and its customers helps you tremendously with integrating into the culture of the company. It will keep you engaged and motivated. Knowing that you help people and improve their lives through the work you do every day can make a world of difference in how you see your job. It gives you sense of accomplishment and helps you take ownership of everything you do in your job.

I spent my second week with a roadside assistance company in one of the call centers to understand the business. I didn't have any experience in this industry. It was a lot to learn and I felt like I was drinking from a fire hose, but what impressed me the most was the dedication and passion of the nearly minimum wage agents. One of the agents, who had been with the company for over seven years, wouldn't stop talking about how much she enjoyed her job and the satisfaction she got from helping people who were stuck on the side of the road or involved in an accident. And she was not the only one who felt that way. Initially, I couldn't understand why these employees who performed such a stressful job were so passionate and dedicated. It couldn't have been just for the paycheck. By the end of my visit, after listening to many live customer calls, I realized that the main reward was the feeling of helping someone in need. The agents communicate with desperate customers, ask questions to understand the problem, and then do whatever it takes to help them.

Going back to the Maslow Hierarchy of Needs, what needs do you think a roadside assistance company satisfied? I would say safety needs. The customers were either involved in an accident or stuck on the side of road, so they were concerned about their safety; I bet they were not thinking about satisfying their esteem or self-actualization needs at that time.

You may not interact with your external customers as closely as these agents were, or you may have no direct contact with them. You do, however, interact every day with your internal customers, and your manager is one of them—the most important one.

READ CUSTOMERS' MINDS

Unless you are psychic, you will never be able to peek into peoples' minds and to know exactly what someone thinks, feels, or really wants. There are some things, however, that can help you at least make a fairly accurate guess, like body language, facial expressions, or tone of voice.

The Perspective Pie (Figure 1.2) has four slices. Each slice helps you get closer and closer to the customers' minds and understand what they need and how you can help solve their problems. Listen to what they have to say and pay attention to what they do. You may not know what they think and how they feel, but put yourself in their shoes. How would you feel; what would you think if you had the same problems or frustrations?

This is an extremely powerful tool that can help you start shifting the focus from you to the customer. The better you understand your customers, the better the chance you have to help them alleviate their frustrations. Start with your current manager and fill each slice of the pie with your best guesses at first. Keep updating it as you learn more and more about your boss and keep the same customer-focused lens on.

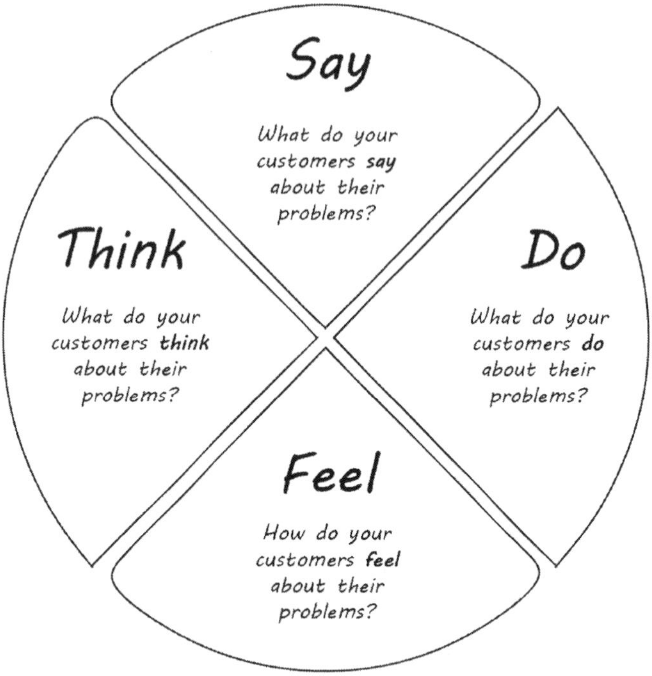

Figure 1.2: The Perspective Pie

Voice of the Customer, Voice of the Business, and Voice of the Employee

Voice of the customer (VOC) is a term that describes your customer's expectations and preferences. It is what customers expect a product to do and how much they are willing to pay. The customer requirements are not always clear or explicitly stated. Usually unwritten needs or wants are also important and have to be translated to specific requirements.

Voice of the business (VOB) represents the needs, wants and beliefs of people who run the business. They are concerned about growth, revenue, profit, and employee satisfaction.

VOC and VOB should always be looked at together. They must be aligned. The customers want the best products at the best prices and the shareholders want to make profit so they can continue to do business. Your job is to help them make that happen.

Voice of the employee (VOE) is crucial to promote the mission of the company because it helps develop ownership and a sense of responsibility. This voice is yours. If you understand the voice of the customer and the voice of the business, you then understand how you directly contribute to the success of your company.

Critical to Customers

To identify and prioritize what is important for you to work on, you first need to understand what motivates your internal customers and what is critical to their satisfaction. These are the expressions of your customer's needs, but they need to be translated into more specific requirements. There are at least two main buckets you should be focusing on.

Critical to quality: What is most critical to customer satisfaction in terms of quality? The customer wants a reliable, defect-free product—it could be an application, a report, or a financial analysis.

Critical to delivery: The customer wants a product delivered on time. In other words, the customer wants you to meet your deadlines. Once you commit to something and agree on a timeline, you must do everything you can to deliver it within that time frame.

Knowing these criteria enables you to drill down deeper and translate them into specific requirements. For example, a defect-free product sounds pretty vague, but if you drill down you may discover more specific attributes. The same applies to delivery. You need to truly understand and translate deliverables into requirements. Develop a detailed timeline and have it approved by customers.

The voice of the customer tells you how well your product/service meets or doesn't meet your customers' needs. But how do you "listen" to their voice? How do you know their expectations?

CTQ Tree

Originally developed as part of Six Sigma Methodology, CTQ Tree (Critical to Quality Tree) is a tool that can be used in many situations, including when you are creating a product or providing a service to your internal customers.

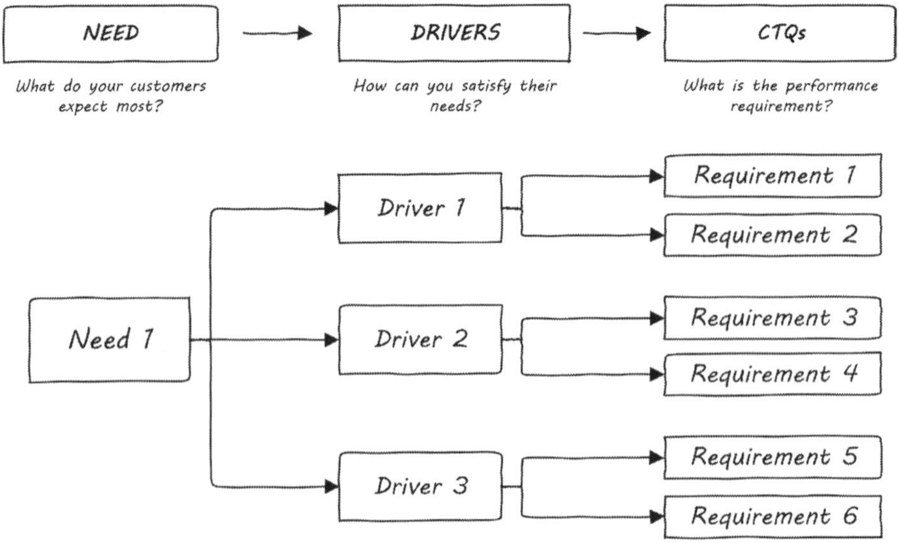

Figure 1.3: CTQ Tree

While we all understand that quality is important to our customers, it is not always easy to define it. This is when the CTQ Tree is useful. It helps you understand how your customers define quality.

Follow these steps to build a CTQ Tree:

Step 1: Identify the needs

The first step is obviously to identify the needs of your customers. I recommend creating a CTQ Tree for every need that you identify. Ask: what is absolutely critical for this product or service? This is not as difficult as it may seem. The easiest way to find out is to ask them. If your customer is your direct manager, just ask him. If your customer is a group of people, you can also organize a brainstorming session using the brainstorming tools you will learn in this book.

Step 2: Identify the drivers

In this step you need to identify what are the quality drivers and how you can satisfy the need. This step is extremely important because these factors determine whether or not the customers perceive your product as high quality. Do not rush through this step. Work closely with your customers to truly understand what is important to them.

Step 3: Identify the requirements

Now that you understand the needs of the customers and what drives quality, you need to identify the performance or criteria to satisfy each of the drivers. Don't be vague. Be specific and use real numbers. State "all requests processed with 24 hours or two business days," not "all requests processed in a timely manner." This step gives you the chance to evaluate whether you have the right skills, resources, or technology in place to meet the requirements. If not, you may need to tap resources from other departments, but the only way to find out is to create specific requirements.

CTQ Tree EXAMPLE

This example illustrates what a company with a call center may need to do to provide outstanding service to its customers when they call the help line.

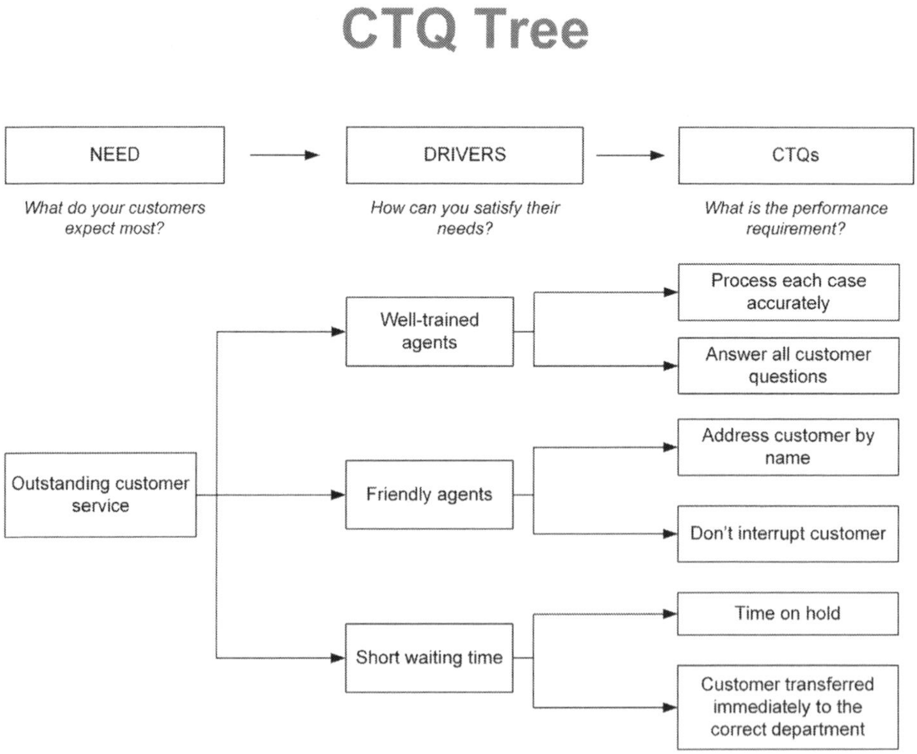

Figure 1.4: CTQ Tree Example

I encourage you to go through this same exercise and use your manager as your customer. What does she or he most expect from you? This tool helps you get specific and identify what you need to do to satisfy your manager's need.

2. TREAT EVERYTHING LIKE A PROJECT

"First, have a definite, clear practical ideal; a goal, an objective.
Second, have the necessary means to achieve your ends; wisdom, money, materials, and methods.
Third, adjust all your means to that end."

\- Aristotle

WHAT ARE YOU WORKING ON?

You are probably thinking "Project? What project? I am not a project manager, I don't work on projects." Yes, you do. I don't mean to intimidate you or to complicate your work, but thinking of your assignments as projects helps you get organized and meet your deadlines. Understanding what and why you are working on something and what are you trying to accomplish are musts before you begin any work. It may be a report, a product, an analysis, or even a bill for a client—you must have a clear understanding of what is expected of you.

Each project begins with a business opportunity as the starting point, but there are many things you need to understand before you begin working on an assignment. If you have managed any type of project, you probably understand the importance of a project charter, regardless of the methodology you used.

Project Charter

The charter is the foundation tool for your project. It must be well-built and solid enough to sustain your project through its lifetime. Even though in certain situations it may seem like overkill, don't skip it and don't underestimate the importance of this tool—it is the synopsis of your project.

Think of the project charter as an anchor, holding you to your initial objective. It must be reviewed and approved by all stakeholders before you begin the work, and it can only be modified if everyone involved is in agreement. My advice is to revisit the charter as you use the other tools in this book, to ensure that everything that you capture still makes sense. Also, use it to make sure that you haven't deviated from your objective and that you are still within the scope of your project.

More often than not, people tend to get carried away and try to solve all the problems of a company in one little project. This leads to scope creep, one of the biggest enemies of your project. It's easy for the scope to expand as the team uncovers potential issues in different areas, but it is your responsibility to keep the team on track and to revisit the charter frequently to ensure that the team is still on the right track.

Now that you understand the importance of this tool, let's review the key elements of a project charter.

Business Case	Why work on the project?
Problem Statement	What is the problem?
Objective	What are you trying to achieve?
Scope	What is in scope and what is out of scope?
Metric	How do you measure success?

Figure 2.1: Key elements of a project charter

Business Case

In this section you will be answering the question: Why am I working on this? "Because my boss asked me to do it" is not an acceptable answer. You must go much deeper and understand the business need. If available, baseline data helps you understand how big of an issue you are facing. A business case identifies the business need of working on a project and it effectively describes the linkage between the project and the strategic goals of the organization. It is important to identify how a project is selected and prioritized among other projects in your organization.

SO, WHAT'S THE PROBLEM?

Problem Statement

Once you understand the circumstances and the business need, ask: "What is the problem?" This is the "so-what" explanation. How is the company or a certain group impacted?

At a minimum, the problem statement should include the description of the defect/problem, the size of the problem and how it is measured, when the problem occurs, and how long it persists. It also helps you understand the conditions in which the problem occurs and the financial impact of the problem.

Project Objective

Now that you have a better understanding of what you will be working on, you can clarify your objective. What are you trying to achieve? What is your goal? Be as specific as possible.

Here are some considerations. Is your goal to just document a certain process, or are you planning to streamline it? Are you going to recommend solutions to address a specific issue, or are you actually going to solve a specific problem? The objective must always be clear, and you should always be able to answer a simple question: what are you trying to achieve?

I remember going to a project team meeting led by one of my direct reports and my boss asked him, "what was the objective of his project?" He seemed puzzled by the question. I had to intervene when he started his answer with "Uh, ah... I think it is." I was so embarrassed, I wanted to hide under the table.

"Setting goals is the first step in turning the invisible into the visible."

-Tony Robbins

You should never hesitate or have to think what the objective of your project is. It must roll off the tip of your tongue. How can you lead a project when you can't even articulate what you are trying to accomplish?

I am sure that you've heard the acronym SMART, especially when you and your manager identify your goals for the year. SMART stands for Specific, Measurable, Attainable, Reasonable, and Time-based. It helps to keep these principles in mind when formulating the objective of your project.

At a minimum, the objective must be consistent with the VOC (voice of the customer), be perfectly aligned with the problem statement, and have an end goal or target—if your goal is, let's say, "to reduce invoice processing time," be specific and state by how much (let's say 50%), or reduce it from 6 minutes to 3 minutes.

Project Scope

In project management, determining the scope of the project is an elaborate process since it refers to the detailed set of deliverables or features of a project. In process improvement, the project scope specifies the boundaries of the project.

A clearly defined scope keeps you and your team focused and motivated. Once you begin working on a project, there is a high risk of scope creep. I've seen this happen often. You will come across processes or different problems that you or someone else believes should be in scope. The project becomes too big and complex and its potential success will be immediately compromised.

I suggest that you clearly spell out in your project charter what is in scope and what is out-of-scope. If you find defining the scope challenging, you can start by identifying what is not in scope, so at least everyone understands what you are not going to address.

Project Metrics

The metrics will allow you to measure the success of the project. How will you know if you in fact improved anything at the end of the project? You have to measure it. A clearly defined project objective can help you identify your metrics.

You may, however, have more than one metric, but I don't recommend more than two: a primary metric and a secondary metric. In my projects, I like to also have a counter metric. For example, if your primary metric is average call time, decreasing it may sound like an improvement, but not if you also decrease customer satisfaction. In this example, a potential counter metric would be customer satisfaction scores. You want to maintain satisfaction at least at current levels, so you don't want to reduce average call time at the expense of customer satisfaction.

You will need to do a before-and-after comparison at the end of the project to see if you made an improvement. Before you start a project, I recommend that you ensure that baseline data is available. Some companies are not very good at capturing and maintaining data, so you may have to collect your own baseline data during the course of the project.

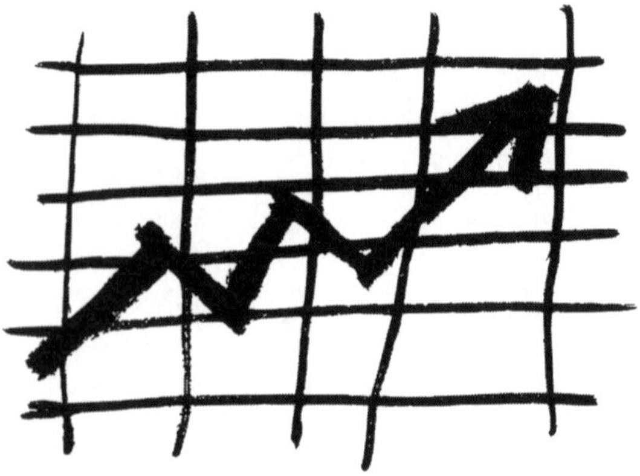

Project Charter EXAMPLE

Project Charter

PROJECT SYNOPSIS		
Project Title:	**Recovery of Advance Fees**	
Project Lead:	Larry Leader	
Project Sponsor:	Sandy Sponsor	
Process Owner:	Olivia Owner	
Cross-functional Resources/SMEs:	*Claims*: Chris; *IT*: Irene; *Product Management*: Paul; *Accounting*: Amy; *FP&A*: Freddy	
Business Case: *Why work on the project?*	At the end of last year, the company has noticed a significant amount of non-recoverable advance fees: - After closing the Client Cloud Tech contract in September, $500k in advance fees were not recoverable; - After the large backlog of credit card transactions in process was resolved, a significant amount of non-recoverable debits was identified in the accrued liability account.	
Problem Statement: *What is the problem?*	There is a growing concern that the company may not able to recover all the advance fees paid to the suppliers on behalf of the clients	
Project Objective(s): *What are we trying to achieve?*	Eliminate non-recoverable advance fees	
PROJECT SCOPE		
In scope:	Transactions with advance fees	
Out-of-scope:	All other transactions	
CURRENT SPECIFICATIONS *What is known about the process?*		
What documentation exists today?	Documented findings as a result of previous closing process	
When and where does the problem occur?	N/A	
How often is the problem happening?	Problem has been happening across the entire portfolio of clients for the past several years	
METRICS		
Primary Metric and Current Value	Unrecovered advance fees as a % of total advance fees	4% (4.5MM) - previous year
Secondary Metric and Value	N/A	

Figure 2.2: Project Charter Example

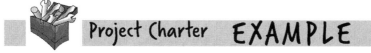

This is an example of a charter for a project to ensure that all the advance fees paid to the suppliers on behalf of the clients are fully recovered. Note that in addition to the key elements shown in Figure 2.2, this example also includes other information like the lead, sponsor, cross-functional team members and the current specifications. Keep in mind that this tool is meant to help you and your team understand what you are working on and why you are working on it. Feel free to add additional information as needed if you find it helpful for the project.

Stakeholder Analysis

Just as it is important to understand what you are working on and what are the expectations of your project, it is also important to understand who your stakeholders are. According to the Project Management Institute (PMI), the term *project stakeholder* refers to "an individual, group, or organization, who may affect, be affected by, or perceive itself to be affected by a decision, activity, or outcome of a project."

Not knowing who to involve, who will be impacted, or who you will need to get approval from, can slow down your project and negatively impact your results.

Most organizations that I have worked for operated in silos. They didn't like to communicate, they didn't want to include the right people from the beginning, and they just wanted to operate in their own sandbox. This is a huge problem. I consider most projects to be cross-functional, because chances are that you will need buy-in, support and approval from others—and help breaking barriers you will most likely encounter along the way.

Do not rely solely on your manager. If you want to stand out, you must be proactive and figure out ways to get other people to collaborate and make things happen. Do not wait for step-by-step directions from your manager.

GET 'EM ON YOUR SIDE

Stakeholder management is critical to the success of any project, but unfortunately, it is often overlooked. There are many benefits to involving stakeholders early on. You can utilize the opinion of subject matter experts; moreover, people are more likely to accept decisions if they are part of the decision-making process. If you also gain support from senior management, they can help you win more resources along the way.

Here are a few easy steps to follow when performing a stakeholder analysis:

Step 1: Identify your stakeholders.

You simply need to brainstorm who your stakeholders are—feel free to ask your manager for help. The stakeholders must be people, not departments. For example, don't just list Marketing. Be specific about who from Marketing. Ultimately you will be communicating with people, not departments.

Step 2: Classify your stakeholders.

Not all stakeholders will be able or willing to help you to the same degree. Some may care about the work you are doing and some may not. Use the matrix in *Figure 2.3.* A person's position in the grid is a good indication of the action you need to take.

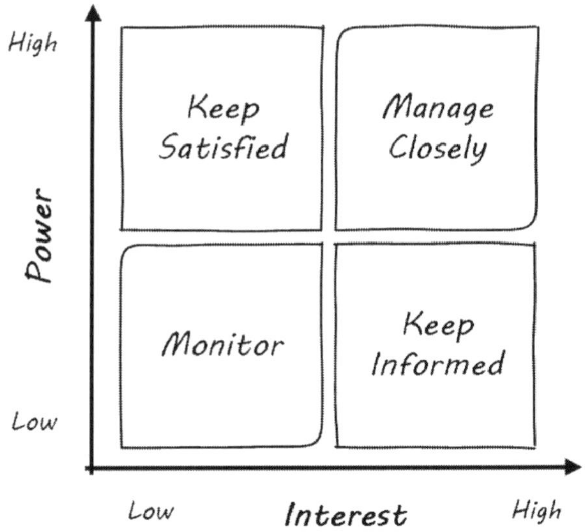

Figure 2.3: Stakeholder Classification

High power, high interest: Fully engage these stakeholders.

High power, low interest: Keep them satisfied, but don't overwhelm them with emails and meeting invites.

Low power, high interest: These are the SMEs (Subject Matter Experts), and the stakeholders that can help you with details such as reports, analysis, or understanding the process.

Low power, low interest: Send occasional communication to keep them informed, but don't bother them with too much information.

Step 3: Learn about your key stakeholders.

You need to understand what level of interest they have in your project, how they prefer to receive communication about the project, whether they are supportive of your project, and if not, what you can to do to win their support. The best way to answer these questions is to talk to them directly and ask them. Most people have no problem sharing their opinion and appreciate the fact that you care about their point of view. This will also help you build stronger relationships.

You may not have easy access to senior management, and if so you can ask your boss to help you. You also need to know what these stakeholders do and how they feel about your project. You can use the tools you learned in the previous chapter.

Stakeholder Name	Communication Approach	How Can Stakeholder Contribute to Project?	What is Important to Stakeholder?	Current Status	Strategy for Engaging Stakeholder
Name	Manage Closely Keep Satisfied Keep Informed Monitor	Expertise Approvals Break Barriers	What does stakeholder want to achieve through the project?	Advocate Supporter Critic Blocker	Team/ One-on-one Meetings Emails

Figure 2.4: Stakeholder Monitoring

If you need to capture more detail and monitor your stakeholders even closer, I recommend using a spreadsheet like the one in *Figure 2.4*. I find it most helpful for larger, high visibility projects, especially if there are high-level executives on your stakeholder list. Your goal is to shift the blockers and critics toward advocates or at least supporters; otherwise, their resistance may slow down your project—like running into a brick wall.

Stakeholder Analysis EXAMPLE

It is unlikely that the CEO, CFO, or even VPs will be part of your stakeholders list, unless you work for a small company or you are part of the senior management team. You must, however, identify all the players that either will be impacted or can help you with the project. Engage them at the beginning of the project, regardless of their function.

Stakeholder Analysis

Stakeholder Name	Communication Approach	How Can Stakeholder Contribute to Project?	What is Important to Stakeholder?	Current Status	Strategy for Engaging Stakeholder
Craig the CEO	Manage closely	Approvals Break barriers	Cost savings, reduction in footprint, timely execution	Advocate	Monthly meeting
Victoria the VP	Keep satisfied	Approvals, facilitating conversations	No disruptions to operations	Supporter	Email monthly meeting minutes
Chris the CFO	Manage closely	Approvals, facilitating conversations	Cost savings, controls	Critic	Monthly meeting
Dan the Director	Keep satisfied	Expertise, approvals, influence engagement	No disruptions to call center operations	Supporter	Email monthly meetings minutes
Susan the Supervisor	Monitor	Expertise	Job security, people are in position for success	Supporter	Emails as needed

Figure 2.5: Stakeholder Analysis Example

RACI Matrix

You probably have noticed how often people who work together on a cross-functional project point fingers and assign blame when things don't get done. This occurs because people tend to assume that someone else is taking care of a particular task or assignment. When the responsibilities are not clear and accountability is ambiguous, uncertainty settles in and this leads to critical gaps in the results.

When dealing with complex projects or when people avoid responsibility, it is extremely helpful to take the time to identify the roles that you and your team members must play in every task. With no clarity on who does what, any project may turn into a frustrating and inefficient experience.

The RACI Matrix is a tool that clarifies the roles that people play within a team. It helps ensure that everything will be completed without duplicating effort.

Deliverable or Activity	Role 1	Role 2	Role 3	Role 4
Deliverable/Activity 1	A	I	R	C
Deliverable/Activity 2	I	C	A/R	I
Deliverable/Activity 3	I	R	I	A

R	Responsible Assigned the work
A	Accountable Makes the final decision and has the ownership
C	Consulted Must be consulted before a decision is made or an action is taken
I	Informed Must be informed when a decision is taken

Figure 2.6: RACI Matrix

Even if you are not the project lead, I encourage you to suggest using the RACI Matrix if the lead doesn't create one. This tool is simple, but people often shy away from it when it comes to assigning responsibilities or accountability.

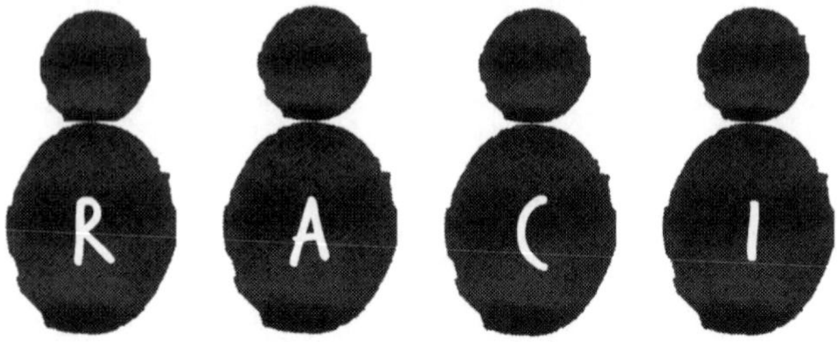

WHO'S DOING WHAT?

Follow these steps to create a RACI Matrix:

Step 1: Identify all the tasks that need to be performed and list them in the first column.

Step 2: Identify all the project roles and list them at the top of the matrix.

Step 3: Complete the chart identifying who has the responsibility (R), the accountability (A), who will be consulted (C), and who will be informed (I) for each task.

Step 4: Ensure that every task has a role responsible and a role accountable for it, keeping in mind that no tasks should have more than one role accountable. You may have more than one person responsible, and ideally multiple people consulted and informed.

Step 5: Share, discuss and agree on the RACI Matrix with your stakeholders before your project starts.

While I prefer creating the RACI during team meetings, it is perfectly fine to create a draft on your own and validate/finalize it with the team. It's crucial, however, for all stakeholders to agree on the roles and responsibilities.

Don't limit the use of a RACI Matrix to the beginning of a project. Use it anytime you or your team members are not sure who does what within a group or department, or even at the end of a process improvement project to clarify who will be implementing the improvements.

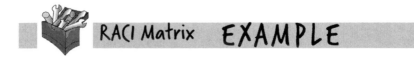

RACI Matrix EXAMPLE

In Figure 2.7, note that for each task there is only one person accountable (A). You may have more than one person responsible (R) and in most cases, you will have more than one person consulted (C) and informed (I). A person could be both accountable and responsible for performing a certain task. While you must always have an A and an R, it is possible to have no Cs or Is, although that is rarely the case.

RACI Matrix

R:	Does the work
A:	Accountable for the work
C:	Consulted as part of work
I:	Informed when the work is completed

STEP	TASK	Joe C	Sid R	Judy O	Chris S	Noah R	Jane S
1	Create current state process map	A	C/I	R	I	I	
2	Run baseline data reports	A	C	R		C	I
3	Identify controls within process	A/R	I	C	I		C
4	Analyze billing variances	A/R	I	R			R/C
5	Provide accounting reports	C/I	A	R/C	I		
6	Update client interface process flows	I	C		A/R		I

Figure 2.7: RACI Matrix Example

3. BROADEN YOUR VIEW

"The important thing is not to stop questioning. Curiosity has its own reason for existing."

—Albert Einstein

BE CURIOUS

Whatever your job is today, you must understand that you are part of large organization. You do not operate in a bubble. The silo mentality of many organizations I worked for in the past is mind-boggling. Why don't people care to understand how their work impacts other areas of the business? Yes, it is wonderful to innovate and come up with great ideas, but if they are not executed properly, they are worth nothing. Developing a product that will not generate any profit due to a saturated market is not going to benefit any company. Promising a client functionality that cannot be built due to system limitations is a recipe for disaster.

The disconnect between Marketing, Sales, Product, or Finance is unhealthy, and happens more often than you would think. And it happens for multiple reasons. Not only when a sales person promises everything the client is looking for to make a sale, or when a product manager comes up with innovative product idea that turns out to be impossible to execute; it happens in general when people on any team don't understand the impact of their actions on other departments. They don't understand, or they don't want to understand, the end-to-end process. They simply don't see the forest for the trees.

Unfortunately, this happens not only between groups; it happens between individuals, and even between individuals in the same group who are sitting across from each other. We have become so self-involved in our everyday lives that we bring the same approach to work. How often do you step back and try to understand how your work impacts others, or how work performed by your colleagues impacts your work? Do you really understand what is upstream and downstream of your work?

The following two simple tools will help you see the big picture, the end-to-end process, rather than being isolated in your own silo. The first one is called a SIPOC, and it helps you understand the process at a very high level.

Once you understand the process at a high level, you can dive in even deeper with the Process Flow Diagram. This will give you a better understanding of the detailed process and who does what in the process. Yes, these are simple tools, but you must have curiosity; it's a prerequisite. You must be willing to see and truly understand the full picture, even if you are just a small part of the process.

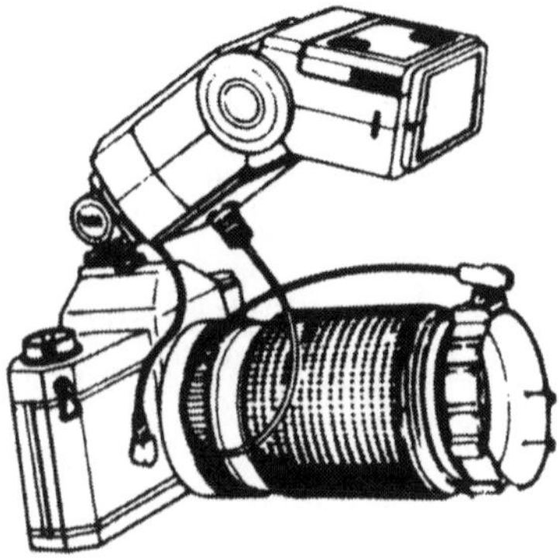

TAKE A QUICK SNAPSHOT

Processes are part of everything we do, and not only at work. You may not realize it, but buying a car, remodeling your kitchen, ordering something online or even grocery shopping are processes—you take a series of actions or steps to achieve a specific purpose. Cooking dinner or baking a cake are also processes. You transform the raw ingredients into ready-to-eat food by following a set of steps like cutting, chopping, and mixing.

Now that you understand why you must see everything you do at work as a process, the following tools will help you represent them visually.

SIPOC

The general purpose of a SIPOC is for project definition and scoping, but you can use this high-level process map to get a quick snapshot of the process. Use it to identify gaps, data collection needs, metrics, and the people involved in the process.

The name of the tool is an acronym of the most important elements of a process:

Suppliers: The providers of the inputs. These are the people, organizations, or systems providing resources to the process—information, materials, or services.

Inputs: Anything that enters the process in order to be transformed: materials, information, and other resources needed to complete the process.

Process: Action steps that transform inputs into outputs.

Outputs: Products or services that result from the process of transforming the inputs.

Customers: Receivers of the output. These are the people, groups, companies, or downstream processes that receive the outputs.

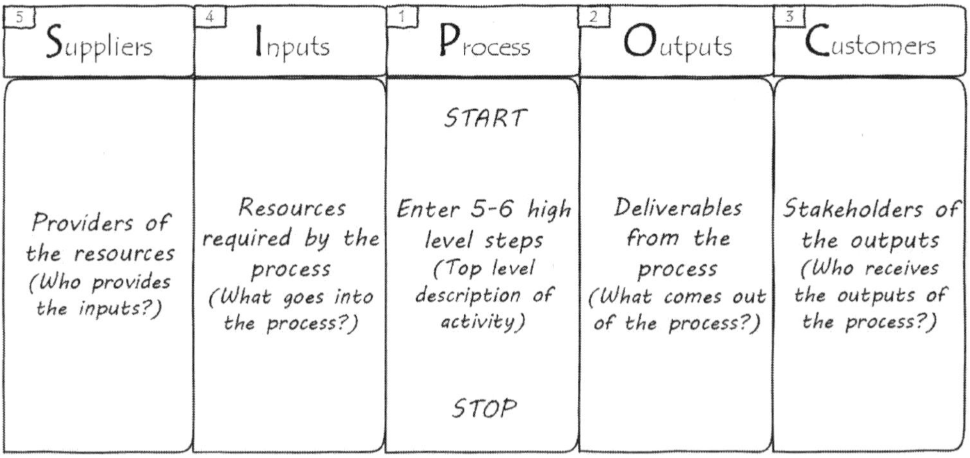
5
Suppliers
4
Inputs
1
Process
2
Outputs
3
Customers
Providers of the resources (Who provides the inputs?)
Resources required by the process (What goes into the process?)
START
Enter 5-6 high level steps (Top level description of activity)
STOP
Deliverables from the process (What comes out of the process?)
Stakeholders of the outputs (Who receives the outputs of the process?)

Figure 3.1: SIPOC

Follow these five steps to build your SIPOC:

Step 1: Identify the steps of the process

Start with the boundaries of the process—where the process starts and where it ends—and then capture 5–6 key steps of the process. Make sure to use action verbs or adjectives to illustrate how the process operates.

Step 2: Determine the outputs of the process

In this section you might list tangible objects or just information, but it is important to use nouns—what does the process produce?

Step 3: List the customers of the process

Who will benefit from the process? Remember to include both internal and external customers.

Step 4: Determine the inputs of the process

The resources used by the process could be capital, information, materials, and even human resources—what needs to be fed into the process to work? You will also use nouns here.

Step 5: Identify and list the suppliers of the inputs

Keep in mind that you may have internal *and* external suppliers. Although it may seem a bit confusing, some of the customers can also be suppliers to the process. You may need data files from the customer to feed into the process. In this case the customer will also be a supplier.

Notice that in steps 2–5 we talked about the process, not about individual steps. Therefore, when identifying the elements of the process, focus on the process as a whole, not on each step individually.

SIPOC EXAMPLE

In the example below, we captured the process at very high level. There are only four steps. If you compare it with process flow in Figure 3.6, you will understand the difference between a high-level process flow and a detailed process flow.

Also note that the bank and the bank customer are listed as both suppliers and customers. The bank customer, for example, is a supplier of the funds since he deposits the money in the bank account, but he is also the one who receives the cash from the ATM—in this case, he becomes a customer/consumer.

SIPOC

SUPPLIERS	INPUTS	PROCESS	OUTPUTS	CUSTOMERS
Providers of the required resources	*Resources required by the process*	*Top level description of the activity*	*Deliverables from the process*	*Stakeholders of the outputs*
		Start		
Bank	ATM Card	Insert card	Returned ATM card	Bank
Bank Customer	ATM	Enter PIN	Updated account balance	Bank customer
ATM Supplier	Available funds	Follow instructions	Cash	
	PIN	Take card, cash, and receipt	Receipt	
		Stop		

Figure 3.2: SIPOC Example

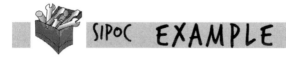

Process Flow Diagram

A process flow diagram is a graphical representation of the steps involved in a process. I find this tool extremely helpful when I need to quickly visualize the steps in a process. Figure 3.2 illustrates a basic process flow. If you need to understand the process in more detail, you may add the functional areas—who does what—and you can also capture the inputs and outputs of each step.

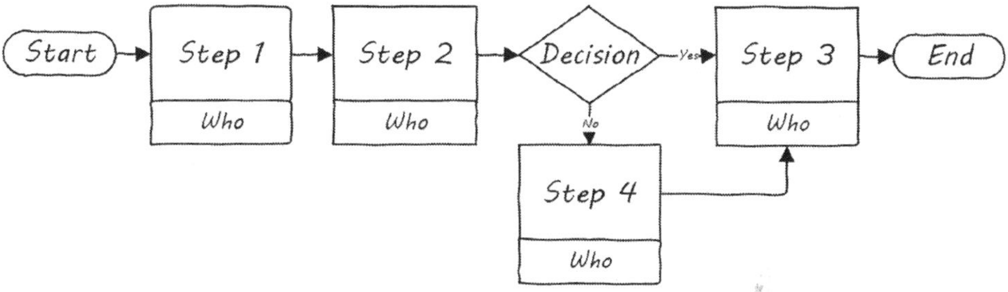

Figure 3.3: Simple Process Flow

There are many reasons for creating a process flow:

1. For documentation

Sometimes the processes are only mapped *in the head* of the person doing the work. This happens more often than you think. I've worked with many people who have done the same job for over twenty years and had no documentation of the processes. And the sad part was that nobody else knew exactly what they were doing. Imagine the consequences of these people leaving their jobs!

2. To streamline a process

Once you map a process, you may notice useless steps, duplication of efforts, or bottlenecks that jump out at you. Highlighting the waste in the process and eliminating it can cut costs or reduce time in a process.

3. For communication or training

Process flows can help when there is a recurring need to train or communicate to others how a process works. I recently worked for a company that had a high turnover rate in its accounting group. Since their documentation was outdated—and in some instances non-existent—the manager had to spend a tremendous amount of time training new hires, coaching them, and answering their questions, since they had no documentation as a reference.

4. For identifying potential causes of a problem

You will learn about root cause analysis tools in future chapters, but the first step is to know the process. You can't identify what is wrong with a process if you don't first understand the process.

ARE WE REALLY DOING ALL THAT?

While documenting a process may seem easy, it is not—not because it is difficult to draw some boxes and lines. It's because we never take the time to view our actions as part of a process.

When I spend time with experienced SMEs (subject matter experts) to map a specific process that they perform, I notice that they frequently find it difficult to articulate the steps in sequential order, even though they have been doing it for many years. And once they start seeing the steps on a white board or on paper, the "aha" moments start pouring in. "Why am I doing all these additional steps? That's really dumb. Wow, so much duplication! Why do we need so many approvals?" You will be surprised by how people react when they see the processes mapped out.

> "If you can't describe what you are doing as a process, you don't know what you are doing."
>
> —W. Edwards Deming

In my experience, more often than not, two people working in the same group, sitting next to each other, will perform the same process in two different ways. Why is that? In most cases the inconsistency is due to a lack of standardized and properly documented processes. If there is no clear direction and up-to-date documentation available, people usually develop their own variation of these processes with their own workarounds.

Lack of communication is an ongoing issue for many organizations. It's much easier to send an email or to ping someone than actually to get up and walk to someone to ask a question or offer advice. Get up and go talk to your coworkers, or pick up the phone, instead of starting an email chain that seems to never end.

Understanding a process from end to end and identifying waste, complexity, and inefficiencies are not the only benefits of process mapping. A process flow can also help you identify sources of variation within the process and understand where process controls are needed.

When creating a process flow, you must make sure that you map what is happening at the present time. Start mapping the current state of a process, not what used to happen in the past or what should be happening in the future. Usually, when people start seeing the first few steps of the process mapped out, they start coming up with ideas for improvement and start mapping what they should be doing. You must start with the "as-is" process.

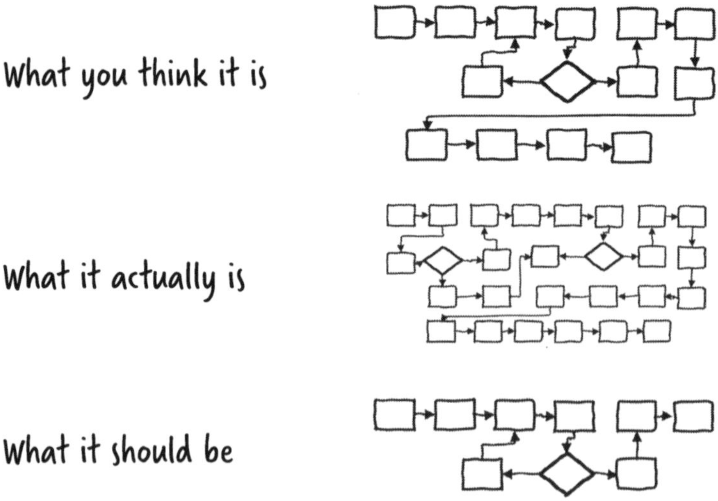

Figure 3.4: Versions of a Process Map

Any process has at least three versions: what you think it is, what it actually is, what it should be (see *Figure 3.4*). When I first learned this in my Six Sigma Black Belt classes, I wasn't quite sure what it meant, but it started to make sense as soon as I mapped my first processes. It will make sense to you sooner than you think.

Follow these steps to create a process flow diagram:

Step 1: Involve the right people

Ideally, include a diverse group of subject matter experts who are involved in the process and can provide insight into the process you are about to map.

Step 2: Clarify the boundaries of the project

You must understand where the process starts and where it ends. If you created a SIPOC, you can use the start and end points from the Process column.

Step 3: Identify each step of the process

Make sure you use action verbs to describe the steps. There are many shapes that you can use, especially if you use a Microsoft Visio. To keep things simple, I recommend that you only use the rectangle shape for the process steps and the diamond for decision points. You may also use an oval shape to mark the start and end of the process.

Step 4: Arrange the steps in order and connect the steps

I recommend drawing the connectors of the steps at the end, after you identified all the steps.

Step 5: List who is performing each step

This step is optional, but it can help you understand any cross-functional involvement in a process. Never use names to identify who is performing a certain task (e.g., use billing manager instead of John). In other words, you are capturing the function performing a certain task, not the people, since they may not even be in the same role the next week.

Step 6: Validate the process flow

After you map the process, you need to make sure that you have captured all the steps and decision points accurately. If you involved multiple people, follow up with them and see if they agree that you got it right.

The biggest mistake you can make when creating a process flow is to assume that you already know the process. Chances are that you don't. It's okay to begin by mapping a process the way you see it, but have other people validate it for you, especially people who do the work. But don't rely on what they tell you.

The best way to understand a process is to "walk the process," which means to sit down with the person performing the tasks so you can observe the process. You may uncover steps that they don't even realize they do.

"Don't believe everything you hear. There are always three sides to a story: yours, theirs, and the truth."

-Unknown

WHAT'S THE VALUE?

Step 7: Perform step analysis

This step is optional; you may not need to get to this level, but it helps to understand its purpose and value. Here you can capture the inputs and outputs of each step—or at least a selected number of steps.

You can also classify the steps into three categories:

Value-Added (VA): Any step in the process that improves a product for the customer (internal or external).

Business Value-Added (BVA): Actions that do not directly increase the quality and value of the product or process and are not apparent to the customer (e.g., regulatory requirement, quality testing).

Non-Value-Added (NVA): Activities that do not contribute to the product or the process and should, therefore, be eliminated. Non-value-added steps are usually considered waste. You will learn more in about waste in the next chapter.

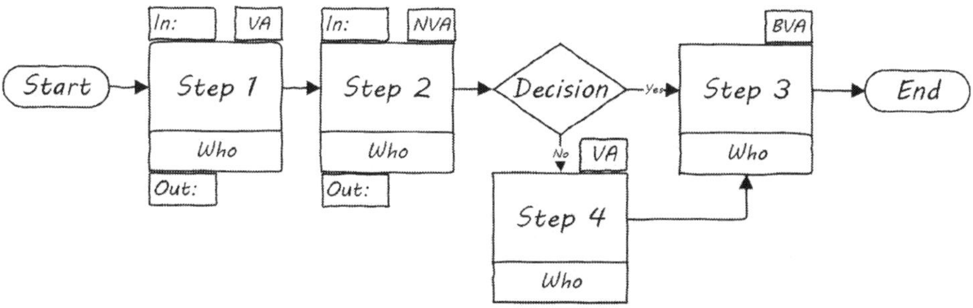

Figure 3.5: Detailed Process Flow

This classification of value is particularly important if your goal is to make suggestions for improving or streamlining a process.

One of the most frequent questions I get, is how much detail to capture in a process flow. If you stay at a high level, you will be missing out on critical details. On the flip side, if you capture massive amounts of detail, your flows will add to the confusion instead of clarifying things.

While I don't have a one-size-fits-all type of answer, I recommend thinking about it the way you think about the water temperature of your shower. You don't want the water to be too hot or too cold. It has to be the right temperature for you, and that temperature is different from person to person. This is true for process flow diagrams. You want just the right amount of detail to help you and the team achieve the goals—not too little, but not too much.

Keep in mind that process flows will not capture key-stroke level detail. That is the purpose of the SOP (Standard Operating Procedures), which is the closest view of the process.

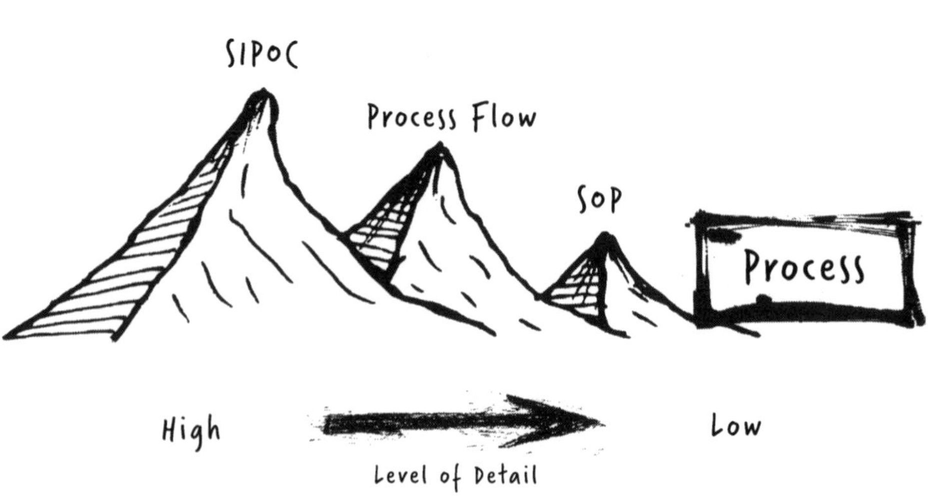

I strongly suggest that you start with mapping the current state of a process ("as-is"). Once you understand the current state, you can use the improvement ideas to create a future state known as the "to-be state." Ideally, this state will be a streamlined process that everyone will follow going forward.

Process Flow Diagram EXAMPLE

Compare the process captured in the SIPOC to this process. This will help you understand the level of detail you need to capture in both instances. Also note that all the steps are interconnected. They all have an arrow going in and an arrow going out—except for the Start and End boxes. Having a box in the middle of the process map without an arrow pointing out stops the flow.

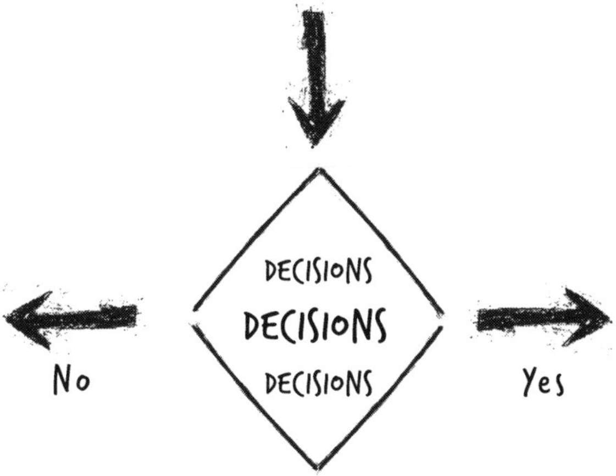

The decision boxes have an Yes arrow and a No arrow. When you use this diamond shape, it implies that a decision is made in that step and you should always have at least two scenarios (e.g., Yes/No). You may also use the box to illustrate multiple options. For example, there could be three ways of communicating with a customer: via email, mail, or text. In this case you could have three arrows (one for each scenario).

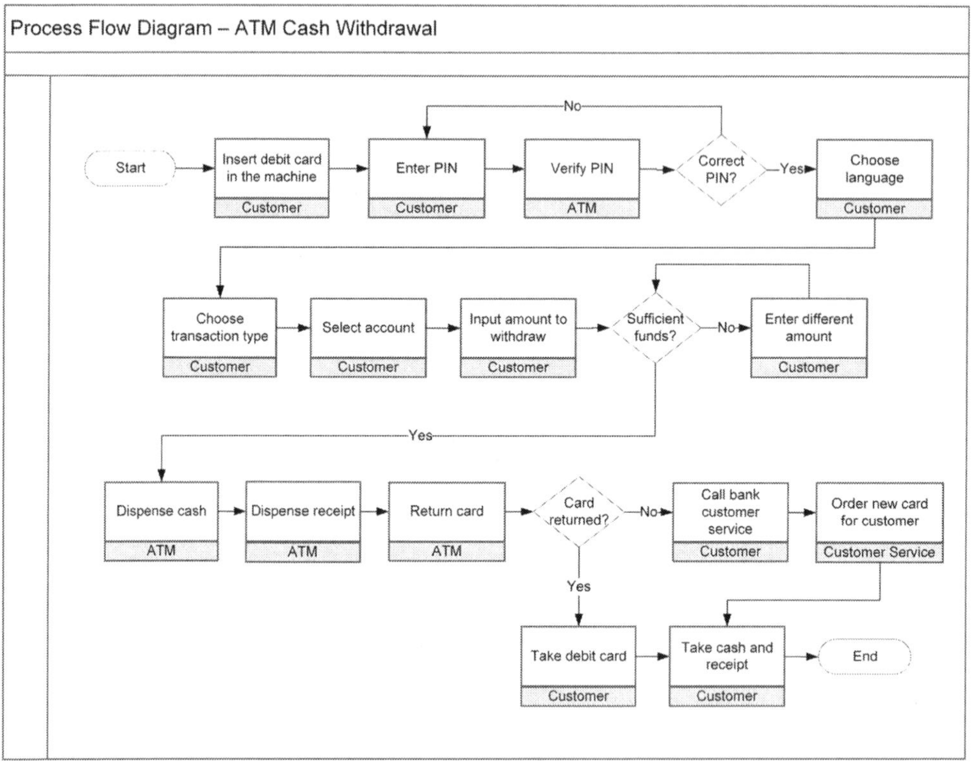

Figure 3.6: Process Flow Example

4. ELIMINATE WASTE

"The most dangerous kind of waste is the waste we do not recognize."

– Shigeo Shingo

I'M TOO BUSY

According to a 2012 study published by the McKinsey Global Institute (MGI), the research arm of management consultancy McKinsey & Company, only 39% of the time we spend at work is on role-specific tasks. So, how about the other 61%? That is the time spent on non-value-added, wasteful activities. I know, you are probably thinking: "Wait a minute, but I am so busy every day! I'm not wasting more than half of my time, am I?" The answer is yes, and you are probably not aware of it.

"It is not enough to be busy, so are the ants. The question is, what are we busy about?" This was a question asked by the famous American writer Henry David Thoreau. How would you answer it?

In his bestselling book *The 4-Hour Workweek*, Tim Ferris has an interesting perspective on time management: "Forget about it." He confesses that it took him a long time to figure out that trying to do more every day and trying to fill every second with some type of work doesn't make sense. The *results-by-volume* approach is "flawed and dumb." Being "too busy" is often used to avoid important but uncomfortable actions. Reorganizing your email, walking through the office to request documents that you don't really need, or checking your smart phone every five minutes are examples of creating busywork.

Busy is not equivalent to productive; it is living in a constant state of being overwhelmed. When people say to me, I know how busy you are, I always want to ask "How do you know?". Guess what? I am actually not that busy. And that is not because I have nothing to do or because I am bored. It's because I am in control of my time. It's because I'm on top of my agenda. Being *too busy* seems to imply *out of control.* When I find myself in a situation to answer a simple "How are you?" with "busy," that is a cue for me to step aside and re-evaluate my priorities. Often, the term *busy* equals a lack of priorities.

I bet that Taiichi Ohno felt the same way when he created the Toyota Production System (TPS). TPS is a Lean Manufacturing framework based on the idea of preserving or increasing value with less work. It's about working smarter, not harder. But how can you achieve better results with less work? By eliminating wasteful activities. And this is not just applicable to manufacturing; waste happens everywhere.

The very first step in eliminating waste, however, is to identify it. In Chapter 3 you learned the importance of understanding the end-to-end process. You also read about how to create detailed process flows. Once you map a process, it will become clearer that some steps waste time or resources.

WHERE'S THE WASTE?

Most of the time, waste is obvious; you don't need to be a Lean expert to recognize it. But this is not always the case. As Ohno said: "Waste is hidden. Do not hide it. Make problems visible."

But what is waste, anyway? Waste is anything that doesn't increase value in the eyes of your customers, both external or internal. It is something that adds no value. Waste is any part of a process that is not required to complete the process successfully and please your customer. If you are not sure if something can be labeled as waste, ask yourself: Is the customer willing to pay for this?

If you are working on a report or a PowerPoint presentation for an upcoming meeting and it is taking you longer than you anticipated, ask yourself if your manager, the shareholders of your company, or the final customers would be happy to pay you for all that work. If the answer is no, you are spending far too much time on that assignment.

Our customers are not happy to pay for our actions that add no value to what they want. If you order a steak cooked medium and it arrives burned, you will probably send it back or order something else. Would you be happy if it shows up on your bill? Would you be happy to pay for it anyway? Of course not. You would want it removed.

"Not adding value is the same as taking it away."

-Seth Godin

When you buy a product in a store, however, it is difficult to determine if the price that you are paying includes costs that you do not want to pay for. Would you be willing to pay for an operator waiting around for the previous steps to complete while checking his phone? How about paying for storage of the product for many months before it is delivered to the store?

There are three optimal ways to address waste: eliminate it, pass it on to the customer by inflating the price of the product, or reduce company profits. Obviously, no company would be happy to take a hit and reduce profits, and if you increase prices the customers may go elsewhere. Therefore, the best way to deal with waste is to eliminate it.

Effectively eliminating waste also increases the profitability of a business. It filters out steps that are not required to deliver a product or service to the customer.

To eliminate waste, it is important to understand what it is and where it resides. Although it was originally created and used in manufacturing, the following Lean waste tool has universal application to businesses today. Waste can be found in any processes, across all industries.

Eight Wastes of Lean

From a Lean perspective, there are eight traditional types of waste: defects, overproduction, transportation, waiting, inventory, motion, overprocessing, and unused intellect.

1. Defects

When you hear the word *waste*, you probably think defects. This is the most obvious of the eight wastes. Quality defects have a direct impact to the bottom line of any company, and unfortunately many are often difficult to detect before reaching customers.

A defect is any process output that does not meet customer requirements. Missing information, product or transactions placed on hold, incorrect data entry and invoice errors are only a few examples of defects.

Preventing defects is better than detection because handling them is costly. Often, they require rework or replacement and this can lead to unhappy and frustrated customers.

2. Overproduction

Producing more than is needed or before it is needed is considered overproduction. This is one of the most harmful wastes since it creates additional waste, including excess inventory—which masks other problems of an organization—and transportation.

The goal should always be to deliver exactly what the customers want exactly when they want it, the philosophy of *Just in Time* (JIT). This is easier said than done, however, and that is why so many companies today operate inefficiently on a *Just in Case* basis.

Some examples of overproduction are: processing low-priority requests before priority requests, producing or delivering sooner than needed, generating extra reports, sending emails to people that don't need to be cc'd, processing an order (which might change) before it is needed, or storing extra copies in redundant filing systems.

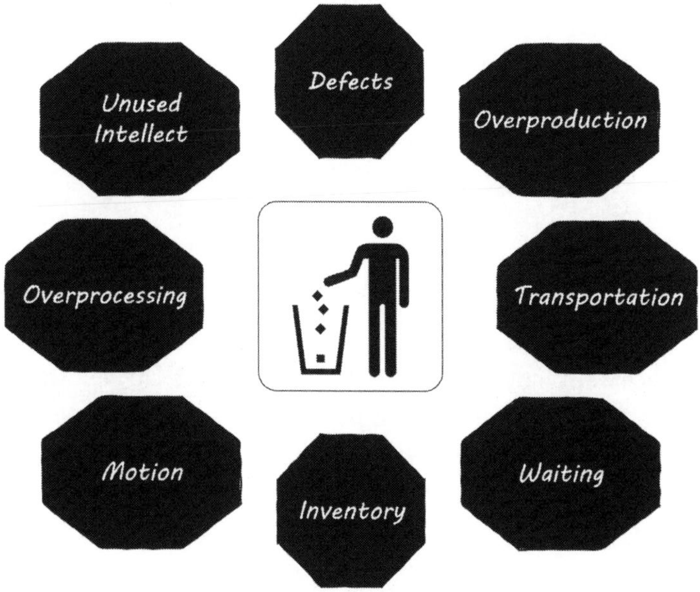

Figure 4.1: The Eight Wastes

3. Transportation

Without transportation, the supermarkets would not receive food, houses would not receive electricity, and we would not receive any mail or emails. Unnecessary movement of products, materials, or information, however, is when transportation becomes waste.

Any material or information handling, movement of paperwork, multiple hand-offs of electronic data, excessive email attachments, chasing of information ("Who has that expense figure?") are a few examples of when transportation becomes waste, because it adds no value to the product.

4. Waiting

How often do you spend time waiting for an answer from a colleague or an approval from a decision-maker so you can move forward in a process? Luckily, now we have smart phones to keep ourselves busy while waiting, but do you think that your customers would be happy to pay for that?

Waiting for the previous step in the process to finish, a slow computer, dependent activities that are not synchronized, waiting for approvals, clarification or correction of work from upstream processes are all wastes and must be eliminated.

5. Inventory

Every piece of inventory that you hold has a physical cost associated with it. Not only is cash tied up in inventory instead of being used elsewhere, but the product has to be moved around, stored, transported, tracked—it may even become obsolete and will be thrown away and written off.

If you don't work in manufacturing or retail, you may ask: "What inventory? We do not produce anything." Yes, you do. Everybody produces something. Piles of anything stuck in your queue is your inventory. Invoices not sent to clients, excess products and materials not being processed, excessive raw, in-process, or finished goods inventory, extra office supplies, unanswered emails, or transaction backlogs are considered waste, as they haven't yet added value to the consumer.

6. Motion

Unnecessary steps to complete a job are also considered waste. Movement of people, machines, or data, excessive steps between operations, shifting back and forth between computer screens, searching for missing information, or shuffling through papers are all waste. Accessing multiple sources to get the information you need because it is not in the expected place, or having to keep scrolling up and down computer screens adds no value in the eyes of the customer, and therefore must be eliminated.

7. Overprocessing

More work or higher quality than is required by the customer is another type of waste, although it may not seem that way. I call this the Lamborghini effect: you build a luxury, super-expensive vehicle, but the customer only wanted a simple method of transportation; perhaps a horse and buggy would have been enough. This may not seem like a big deal, but it is, because that was not what the customer wanted and he will not pay for it.

Any effort which adds no value to a product or service or makes enhancements “invisible” to the customer, such as re-entering data into multiple information systems and generating unused reports are prime examples of overprocessing. I see this type of waste all the time, especially when new employees try to impress their colleagues and managers.

8. Unused Intellect

Under-utilizing employee skills and knowledge is an issue that many companies fail to address. We all tend to operate in a limited environment and we don’t even notice or care what our co-workers think—or we don’t even realize how much they can help us with their knowledge and experience.

Not valuing employees who are involved first-hand with the actual work, not listening to employees’ complaints/suggestions, not matching employees’ skills to assigned tasks, all become a waste of talent of the people within an organization.

WASTE OF TIME

Another common type of waste is interruptions. It’s so easy to get distracted these days. I don’t know about you, but when I am in the office I get interrupted frequently and I find it very hard to quickly return to what I was doing. You will learn more about prioritizing and staying focused in Chapter 6, but for now it is important to realize that distractions and interruptions are the biggest type of waste in today’s workplace and must be eliminated: the waste of time.

In *The 4-Hour Workweek*, Tim Ferris defines interruption as “anything that prevents the start-to-finish completion of a critical task." He identifies three major types of interruptions:

Time wasters: things that can be ignored with no severe consequences, like unimportant emails and phone calls, web surfing, or irrelevant discussions.

Time consumers: requests or tasks that need to be completed eventually—like responding to emails, returning phone calls, or running personal errands—but that interrupt high-level work.

Empowerment failures: situations when someone needs approval to accomplish something simple—fixing a small customer problem, responding to a customer, or cash expenditures under a certain amount.

"Re-improve what was improved for further improvement."

–Taiichi Ohno

Regardless of the type, identifying and recognizing waste is a critical first step. Eliminating it is the next step, and it can be done with the help of the tools in this book. Once you develop an eye for waste, you will notice it everywhere, and you will realize that is a continuous process. It's called "continuous improvement."

Streamlining and re-designing will lead to more efficient processes and result in the reduction of waste. I have seen many organizations spend a fortune on software, hoping that automation will make the waste disappear. That is rarely the case. What usually happens is that they automate wasteful processes without even taking the time to understand and streamline them first. The final result is an expensive, yet automated, messy process.

5. BRING SOLUTIONS, NOT PROBLEMS

"Don't find fault, find a remedy".

– Henry Ford

PROBLEMS ARE LIKE GOLD MINES

It drives me absolutely crazy when my direct reports come to me with problems, and just drop them on me and leave. It's like saying: "Here is another problem, it sucks to be you, but you get paid the big bucks." What am I supposed to do?

If you manage people, I am sure that this happens to you and that you are probably as frustrated as I am. I would not expect them to come to me with clear solutions, but as a manager, I rely on my people to help me solve problems, not just to point them out. I am their customer, after all.

When organizations decide to create a new position, or to hire someone to replace a vacant role, it's because they have a need to be fulfilled. They are willing to invest in people to help solve their problems, not just bring them to their attention. It's like hiring a plumber to fix your leaking sink and when he sees that a pipe is rusted and needs to be replaced, he just lets you know that your pipe is rusted and leaves. Wouldn't you expect him to fix it, or at least advise you on the next steps?

Maybe I am crazy, but I view problems as gold mines. They are great opportunities for us to shine and make an impact, and luckily, they are everywhere. Once you identify that something is not going as planned or you detect specific issues, complaining to your manager is not going to solve anything.

You must resist the temptation to rush into your manager's office to tell her that something is wrong. You need to prepare first. What do you think could be causing the problem? What would you do about it if you were the manager? If you can go to your manager with at least some proposed approach on how to solve a problem or with some ideas of what potentially caused it, you will be a hero, I promise.

Go Beyond Symptoms

Wouldn't it be nice if you could easily identify the root cause of a problem? Even though we feel like we know what is causing a problem, most of the time it is the symptom of an underlying cause.

Imagine having severe back pain on and off for many weeks and the doctor tells you to take pain medicine. After finishing a bottle of ibuprofen, the pain keeps coming back, so the approach didn't really help. You go to another doctor for a second opinion and it turns out that the pain was in fact caused by a kidney stone. So, because you were attempting to treat the back pain—which was just a symptom—the pain kept coming back. The root cause of the pain was actually the kidney stone, and once addressed, the pain finally will go away for good.

Now that you understand the difference between a symptom and a root cause, you can use the simple tools in this chapter to help you get to the root cause of a problem much faster. But before we get there, let's spend a few minutes introducing the famous nine-dot puzzle.

Nine-dot Puzzle

This exercise may be familiar to some of you. It asks you to connect all nine dots with four straight lines without lifting the pen from the paper. If you have never seen this exercise, I encourage you to try it before you turn the page.

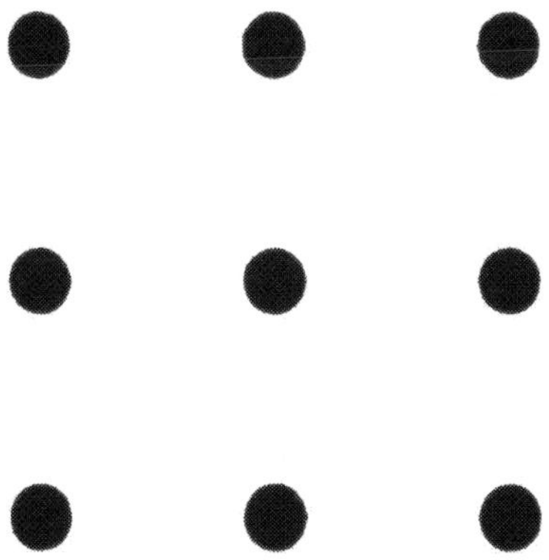

Figure 5.1: Nine-dot Puzzle

Many years ago, when I first played this game during a management training class, I found myself trying to solve it inside the space of the dots, as though the outer dots were the outside limits of the puzzle. Although the instructions were clear, I assumed that I had to stay within the square formed by the outer dots. I was not the only one struggling to solve it.

After a few minutes, the instructor gave us a hint: "Feel free to use the entire sheet of paper." That changed everything in an instant. It was like a new world of possibility opened to us.

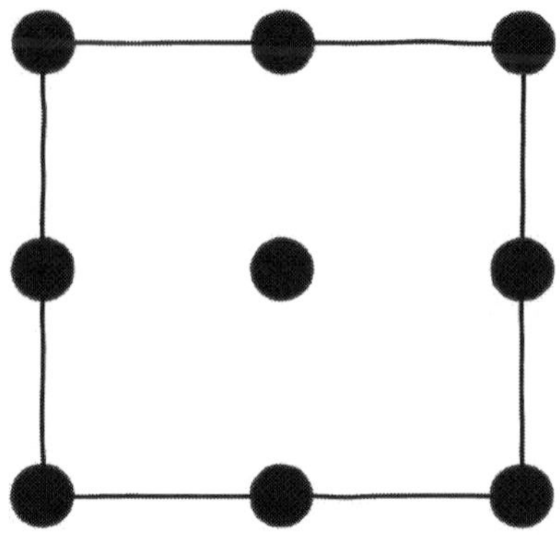

I find it interesting how our minds are able to solve certain complex problem effortlessly, yet we struggle to solve problems that require "out of the box" thinking. This exercise is a powerful example of thinking creatively, and it confirms why the catchphrase "think outside the box" has become a metaphor that is widely used in many business environments today. It encourages us to think differently, unconventionally, and from a new perspective.

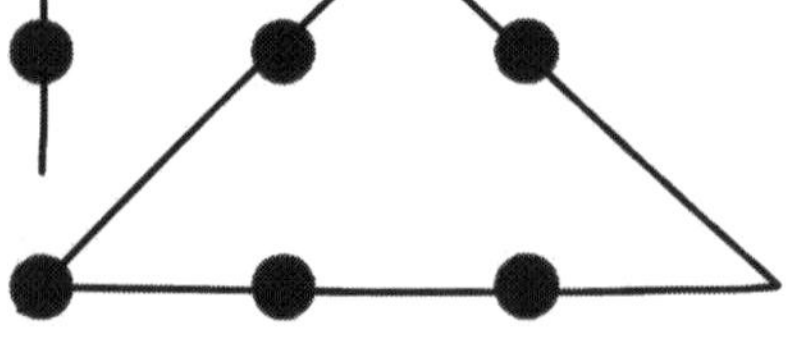

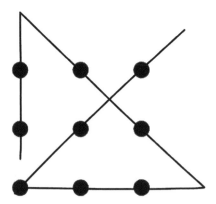

Figure 5.2: Nine-dot Puzzle Solution

Brainstorming

Brainstorming is an effective tool to mine ideas from your mind. The term *brainstorming* was first used by an advertising executive, Alex Osborn, in the 1950s to describe a specific technique when a group of people get together to generate ideas—just come up with as many ideas as possible and don't worry if they seem too crazy. This activity can be used for many reasons: to come up with new product ideas, improvement opportunities, cost savings, or identifying the root cause of a problem.

Traditionally, brainstorming is a group activity. I have conducted many brainstorming sessions following these guidelines—always brainstorm as a group, encourage people to be open-minded, don't criticize, and build on other people's ideas.

While I think that these activities do help generate interesting ideas, I found that as soon as someone comes up with an idea, the rest of the group tends to limit themselves and they think similarly about the problem. I also noticed that reserved and quieter participants can be intimidated by strong personalities and egos and don't come up with any ideas. People are not likely to share their ideas if they feel threatened or intimidated. In fact, according to an article published by *Harvard Business Review* in May 2017, decades of studies demonstrate that group brainstorming generates fewer ideas—and fewer good ones—than individual brainstorming.

Even though it sounds like people can be more creative when they brainstorm on their own, rather than in groups, I am not advocating for individual brainstorming over group brainstorming. I think they both help, especially when you are trying to solve a specific problem. What I think is important is that a brainstorming session must be organized and structured properly, because if it lacks structure, a group session in particular can get off track quickly.

Fishbone Diagram

It's tempting to jump to solutions, but first you need to explore all the things that might cause the problem. Also known as the Cause-and-Effect or Ishikawa Diagram, the Fishbone can help you add structure to a brainstorming session. It also forces you and the team to focus on causes, not on symptoms, and helps you stay focused on a specific problem. This tool combines brainstorming with mind mapping to push you beyond the obvious causes and to help you identify all potential causes of a problem.

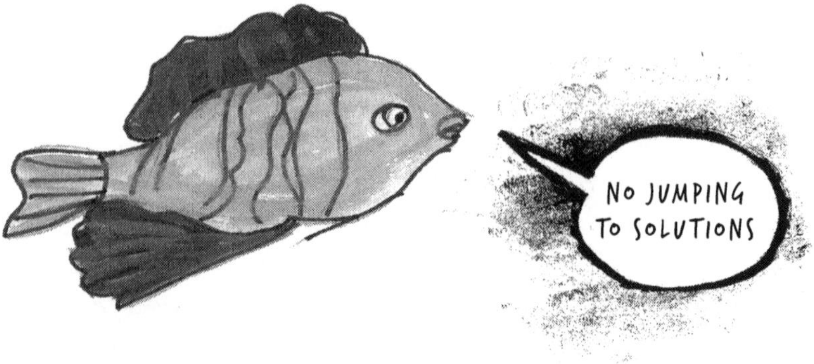

The Fishbone was originally developed in the 1960s by Professor Ishikawa as a quality control tool. It's called "the Fishbone" because it resembles the skeleton of a fish.

You can use the tool in many ways, but the most common one is to help you identify potential root causes of a problem. You can also use it for troubleshooting, risk assessment, identifying improvement opportunities, or understanding the requirements of a process.

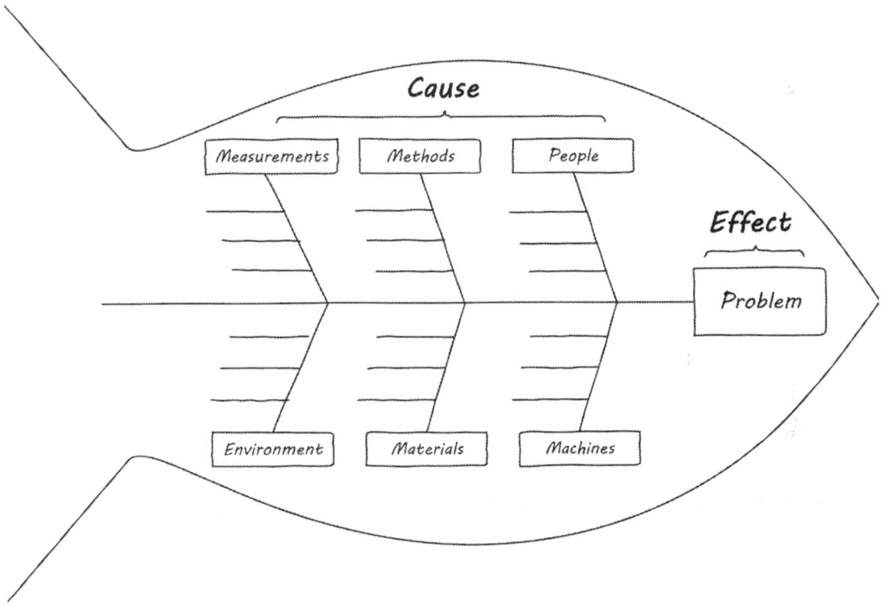

Figure 5.3: Fishbone Diagram

Follow these steps to create a Fishbone diagram:

Step 1: Identify the problem you are trying to solve and write it in the "head" of the fish

If you created a project charter as in Chapter 2, you can use the problem you wrote in the problem statement section.

Step 2: Label the "bones" of the fish

These are the main categories that you will be focusing on. *Figure 5.3* illustrates an example of the traditional categories: People, Methods, Measurements, Machines, Materials, and Environment. You may use other categories depending of the problem you are trying to solve, like the Four Ps of Marketing, for example (Product, Place, Price, and Promotion).

Step 3: Brainstorm potential causes for each of the categories

Write these potential causes on the shorter bones of the fish. If you are not sure under which category a potential cause falls, don't worry. Don't waste time debating it; just add it to one of the likely categories. As long as you capture all the potential causes, you will be fine. The categories are only for guidance.

Step 4: Analyze the diagram

Now that you have identified the potential causes, you circle the most critical ones and investigate them further. This will help lead you to the root cause of the problem.

Keep in mind that all the causes identified in the Fishbone Diagram are immediate causes, *not* root causes. The Five Whys is another simple tool that can help you dig deeper and get to the root cause of a problem.

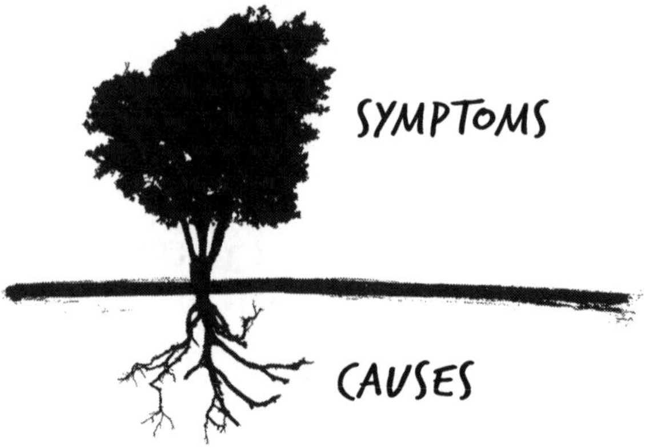

Fishbone Diagram EXAMPLE

This example is related to the Project Charter shown in Chapter 2, Figure 2.2. A team is trying to eliminate non-recoverable fees and the example shows how the team used the tool to brainstorm what could potentially cause some of the advance fees to be unrecoverable. The problem is stated in the head of the fish while the large bones represent six major categories. The smaller bones are potential causes captured during brainstorming.

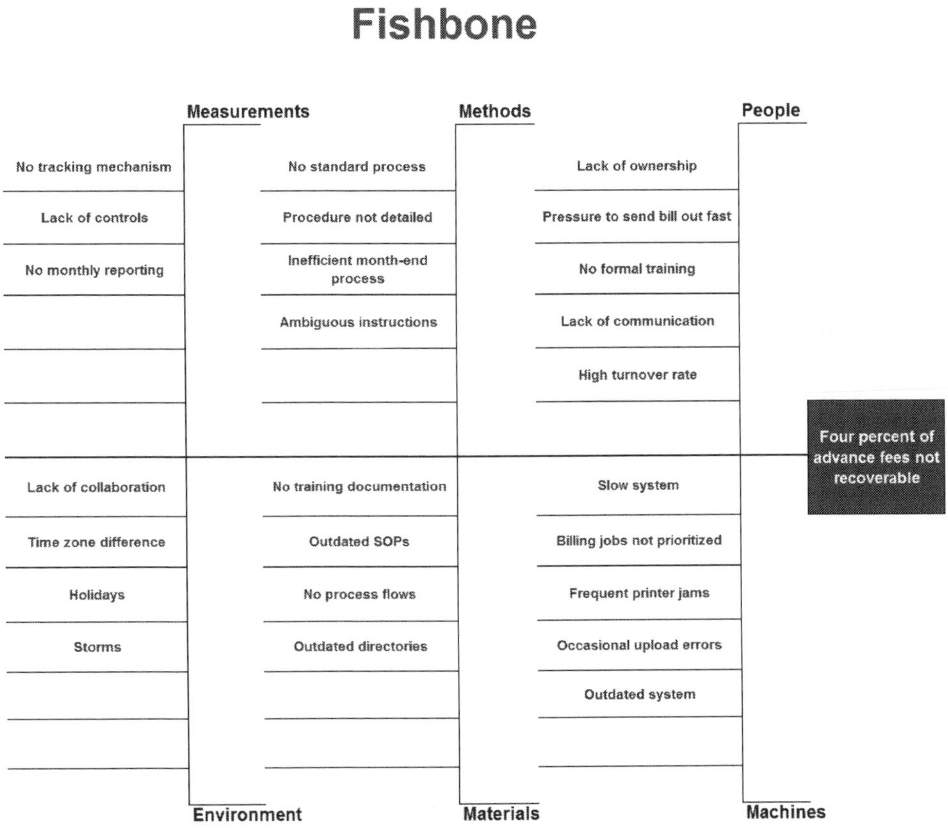

Figure 5.4: Fishbone Diagram Example

When you use this tool, you may change the categories so that they make sense for your project. Teams often spend a lot of time arguing over a potential cause belonging in one category versus other. It doesn't really matter. The categories add structure to the tool. Just make sure that you capture everything, even if you write it under the wrong category.

Five Whys Analysis

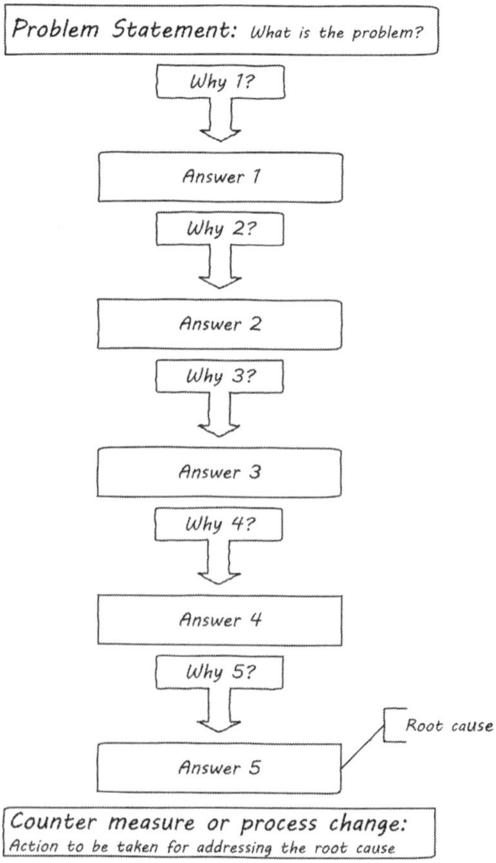

Figure 5.5: Five Whys

If you ever experience problems that you thought you had solved but are stubborn and keep coming back, chances are that you addressed just the symptoms of deeper issues. This happens all the time. We want to fix things fast and we look for quick fixes without realizing that if we don't tackle the real causes, the problems keep coming back. These bandages are just temporary solutions; they are superficial, and they address only the surface issues.

FIND THE ROOT CAUSE

The Five Whys is a problem-solving tool that you can use to dig deeper and move past symptoms to get to the root causes of a problem.

Follow these steps to perform a Five Whys analysis:

Step 1: Define the problem and write it down

Just like the Fishbone, you must be specific and write down the problem statement. This will help you stay focused on one clear problem.

A problem clearly stated is a
problem half solved.

Step 2: Ask Why the problem happens and write down the answer

You will sound like an annoying child in the beginning and some people may perceive you as arrogant because you are questioning them, but don't worry. Just be honest and explain to them that you are trying to identify the root cause.

Step 3: Keep asking Why four more times and write down the answers

I found that people often are not sure when to stop asking why. As a rule of thumb, when you can't go any further because asking *Why* doesn't make sense anymore and it triggers a "just because" answer, you have identified the root causes.

In some instances, the answer to the last question may be something that you can't control—laws and regulations, acts of God, etc. In this case you may go to the previous answer. Keep in mind that you don't always have to ask why five times. Sometimes you can come to root cause sooner, after three or four whys, or you may have to keep asking a sixth or seventh why.

Step 4: Brainstorm solutions and actions

Now that you have identified the root causes, you should come up with ideas on how to address the issues and solve the problem. It is important to focus on counter-measures that will prevent the problem from recurring.

Five Whys EXAMPLE

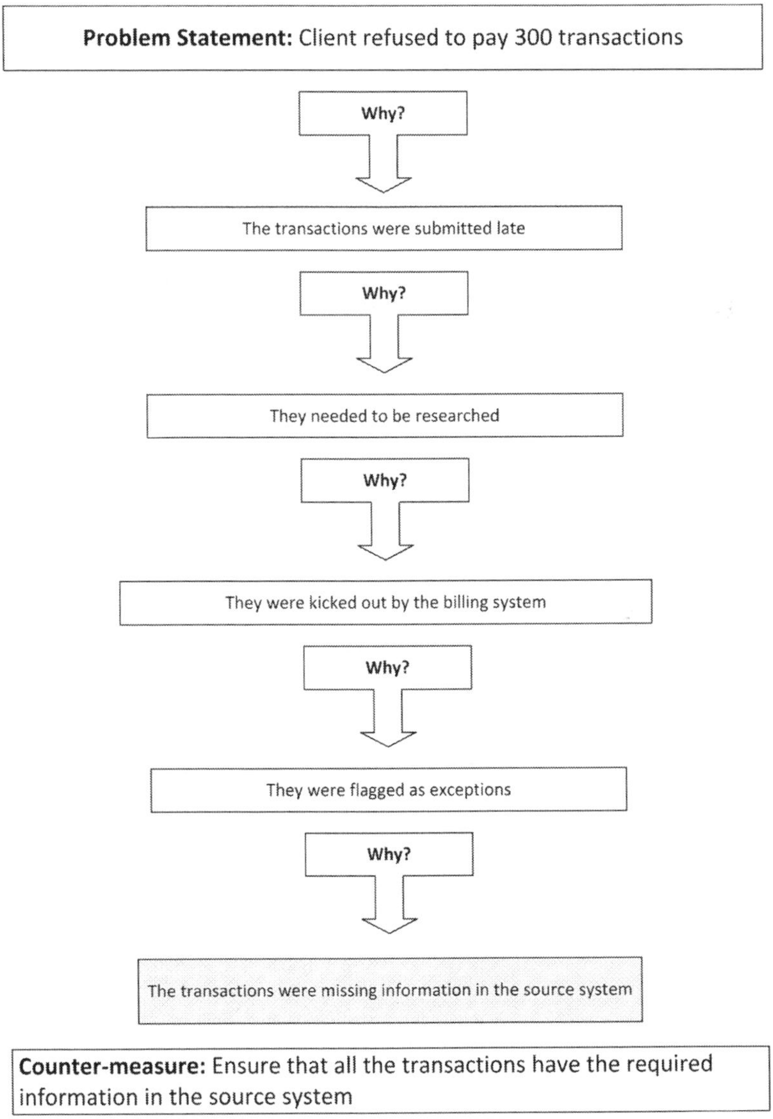
Problem Statement: Client refused to pay 300 transactions
Why?
The transactions were submitted late
Why?
They needed to be researched
Why?
They were kicked out by the billing system
Why?
They were flagged as exceptions
Why?
The transactions were missing information in the source system
Counter-measure: Ensure that all the transactions have the required information in the source system

Figure 5.6: Five Whys Example

In the example above, the client rejected 300 transactions because they were submitted for payment outside the 60-day agreed-upon window. Suppose that you used the Five Whys to identify what caused the issue so you can fix it and prevent it from happening again. What would have happened if you had stopped after asking Why only two times? You would have probably concluded that the client didn't pay the 300 transactions because the research took a long time and this delayed the submission of the invoice. So, naturally, you would have had to speed up the process and perhaps allocate more resources.

The problem with this approach is that this is not a root cause; it is a symptom. The root cause is the missing information in the source system. You need to focus on uploading all the required data. Until you address the root cause, the problem will keep coming back and the customer will keep rejecting invoices. You may go even further and ask Why again and again to understand why the information is missing from the source system. Do not stop at the fifth Why if you believe that you haven't uncovered the root cause yet.

"If I had an hour to solve a problem I'd spend 55 minutes thinking about the problem and 5 minutes thinking about solutions."

-Albert Einstein

6. PRIORITIZE AND FOCUS ON WHAT MATTERS MOST

"There is an art to clearing away the clutter and focusing on what matters most. It is simple and it is transferable. It just requires the courage to take a different approach."

– George Anders

WAR ON DISTRACTIONS

Smart phones, watches, tablets, and frequent breaking news make it almost impossible to get organized and stay focused. And if it happens that you work in a modern open-floor layout where you have to listen to endless conversations around you and people chewing on their fragrant meals or slurping their coffees, you are exposed to a lot of distractions. You get to a point when you feel exhausted without accomplishing much. If you add all the emails and other requests from your peers and your manager, how do you know what to work on and where to begin?

While you can't control the noise and the distractions, you can definitely control your own environment, your working space. Whether it is a cubicle, a desk, or an office, it doesn't really make a difference. You must create an environment that is inviting, clean, and clutter-free so it's easier for you to concentrate and stay focused on your work. A messy, unorganized desk or a dirty laptop or mouse may not seem like a big deal, but it really is, especially if you want to be productive and to focus. If you are disorganized, not only do you spend a lot of time searching for the resources that you need to get the job done, but you also project a negative self-image to your colleagues.

I remember how shocked I was when I first saw the cubicle of a co-worker at one of my companies—filled with piles of paper, files, supplies, topped with dusty Christmas decorations and family pictures including their dogs and cats. A total mess! I immediately thought how difficult it must be to focus and to be productive, since finding anything in those piles was nearly impossible. And here is the best part: this person was a senior project manager. Seeing the state of this office naturally made me doubt the occupant's project management skills.

While project management may not be rocket science, it takes discipline and organizational skills. How can people trust you with their projects when they see how messy your desk is? It's a known fact that not being organized wastes time and lowers productivity.

5S System

Spending time reorganizing your working space is without doubt time well spent. Even small improvements can have a positive impact on your focus, motivation, and productivity.

The 5S System was originally developed for Lean manufacturing as a process for creating and maintaining an organized, clean, and safe workplace. It originated at Toyota as part of TPS (Toyota Production System) in the mid-20th century and since then has proven useful for many industries.

A messy, cluttered workspace can lead to mistakes, slowdowns, and even accidents, and can negatively impact any company in any industry, not just manufacturing. As a result, during the past few decades, 5S became a method for reducing waste and improving efficiency and productivity in any space, whether it is an office, a desk, or a large manufacturing facility.

Increased productivity, reduced costs, and higher work quality are only a few of the benefits of 5S. A neat, clean, and organized working place makes a dramatic difference to any work environment. In fact, it makes a difference even in your own home; the principles of 5S can also apply to your computer folders and your email.

In short, 5S means assessing everything that you have in a space, eliminating what is unnecessary and organizing things logically so they can be found when needed. The trick is to keep the cycle going—organize, clean, repeat.

I believe that regularly cleaning and maintaining a clutter-free workspace has many benefits. It's easy to make excuses: "I don't have time for it," or "nobody cares anyway," or "it will get messy again." But there are many reasons to do it. First and foremost, it can give you a sense of ownership of the space, which will help you in the long run to be more invested in your work and your company. Second, it cultivates mental discipline that will not only help you appreciate a neat workspace, but will also create a positive image of you for your manager and colleagues. Little things *do* matter in life.

TIME TO TIDY UP

So, what are the 5 Ss? 5S was based on an organization system that contained 5 words that begin with the letter S. Since it originated at Toyota, the original words were in Japanese, and had to be adapted to English. The Japanese words (Seiri, Seiton, Seiso, Seiketsu, and Shitsuke) were adapted to English as: Sort, Straighten, Shine, Standardize, and Sustain. Sometimes the 5S system is referred to as 5S+1 or 6S. The sixth S stands for Safety. It has been added more recently;

it is also critical to integrate safety into all of the other S's. Let's look at each of them individually and understand what they mean.

Figure 6.1: The Five Ss

Sort

The first step of 5S involves going through all your folders, loose papers and supplies in your work area to determine what needs to be present and what can be removed. Some questions to ask yourself during this phase are: What is the purpose of this item? How frequently do I use it? When was the last time I used it? Does it really need to stay here?

Chances are that you won't even remember the last time you used most items in your working space. These questions will help you determine the value of each item, which items are necessary, and which ones just take up space. You probably don't even need most of them anymore. Remember, your workspace includes what is in your drawers. You will identify paperwork that you don't need to keep, and supplies that you are not going to use in the next few months. It will take longer than you think to go through ten notebooks or a few dozen pens and pencils.

This also applies to papers hanging on your walls and other artifacts that take up space and can interfere with your ability to stay focused.

It's okay to have a couple of pictures of your spouse, children, or pets. But please, do not display an entire album of family pictures. This is a workplace, and people don't really care about your cute cat named Fluffy anyway. All these photos make your desk look messy and distracting.

Once you go through everything and identify objects that you don't use every day or you haven't used in a while, you must decide what to do with them. For items that you use at least once per day, keep within reach. Place items that you use at least once a week in a drawer or a file cabinet close by. For seldom-used items, place them in a storage area or feel free to throw them away.

If you are not sure if certain documentation is still needed, check your company's or department's retention policy. Some documents may have to be kept for a certain amount of time for regulatory or audit purposes.

Straighten

Once you get rid of the clutter, it will be much easier to organize everything and ensure that every item is easy to find and in an optimal location. Here are some questions to ask yourself: Which items do I use more frequently? Where is the most logical place for each item so I avoid unnecessary motion? The tasks you perform and the frequency of those tasks will help answer these questions.

If you have a file cabinet with multiple drawers, it helps to label each section and each folder so that you know what it is in each of them. Don't go overboard with labeling.

I remember when a former employer was implementing 5S, and they had us label the places for the keyboard, mouse, stapler, and telephone. That was overkill, and everyone found it strange. Don't go to this extreme. Keep in mind that the purpose of this exercise is to help you stay organized and find things more easily, not to create unnecessary work.

Shine

The third S of the 5Ss stands for Shine, and it is focused on cleaning up your workspace. Yes, it involves physical cleaning, like dusting and wiping your desk and your shelves. Cleaning your workspace may not sound exciting, but it is very important. When you get busy, housekeeping is often overlooked. Who has time to clean? Do not leave it up to the janitorial staff. It's your responsibility to keep your work area clean. In addition to basic cleaning, Shine also involves performing regular maintenance on any equipment that you use. By performing regular maintenance, you can catch problems and prevent breakdowns in the future.

Standardize

Once the first 3Ss are completed and things look good, all the clutter is gone and everything is organized, it is time for *you* to shine. Once you go through this exercise, you will start to notice how messy other workspaces are. Take the initiative and coordinate a 5S event for your group, department or organization. Talk to your manager and explain the importance of a clean and organized workplace and ask for support on coordinating a 5S event.

Unfortunately, when the 5S concept is new to a group, getting cleaner and more organized may excite everyone in the beginning, but people will slowly start sliding back to the way they were. Standardizing helps turn one-time efforts into habits, and sets apart 5S from just a spring cleaning activity. You can use *Standardize* to assign tasks and responsibilities to people in the group and to create a recurring schedule to make sure that all these activities become routines. I find visuals like posters, signs, and labels to be helpful.

Sustain

Sustain means keeping 5S running. Once everything is clean and organized and standardized procedures are in place, and once you have a set schedule for performing the activities, you must ensure that things don't pile up and get dusty again. Now that you have a place for everything, ensure that everything is in its place and that it stays in its place. This can be gradually embedded in the culture of your group and even your organization, and then everyone will benefit and start seeing positive results.

Safety

As I mentioned earlier in this chapter, some companies, especially in the manufacturing industry, like to include a sixth S in their 5S program: Safety. When *Safety* is included, the system is often called 6S or 5S+1. Typically, this step focuses on what can be done to reduce accident risks in the workplace.

> "The safety of the people shall be the highest law."
>
> –Marcus Tullius Cicero

You must keep safety in mind as a top priority. If you notice any potential hazard in your office, inform your manager immediately; don't worry about the other Ss at this point. Safety always comes first. A misplaced cord, a loose cable, supplies stacked or stored improperly or anything that could cause an injury are all potential hazards and must be eliminated immediately.

Accidents do happen occasionally. Now that you understand the 5S principles, ask yourself: how could less clutter, cleaner surfaces, or better signage have helped prevent the accident?

PRIORITIZE

From time to time we may feel overwhelmed by all the items on our to-do lists and we often hear that prioritizing is the key to getting more organized and determining what is most important. But how do you know what is most important? And important to whom? The following tool, called *The Cause and Effect Matrix*, will help you prioritize your tasks and work on what matters most to your customer, manager, or other stakeholders.

C&E Matrix

Traditionally, a Cause and Effect Matrix (in short, C&E matrix) is used to help identify which factors affect the outcome of a Lean Six Sigma project. It is a prioritizing tool that helps you correlate how important certain inputs (Xs) are relative to achieving certain outputs (Ys). Although it is a bit more complex than other tools described in this book, the C&E Matrix is a powerful tool that can be used any time to prioritize what you need to work on. Once you understand how it works, you can apply it to many aspects of your job, and even to your personal life.

The C&E Matrix can also help you discover the most influential factors that truly add value to your customers, especially when you feel overwhelmed by your to-do list.

Importance to Customer	9	1	9	3	
Customer Requirements / Inputs	Req. 1	Req. 2	Req. 3	Req. 4	Total
Input 1	3 9x3=27 +	0 1x0=0 +	9 9x9=81 +	1 3x1=3 =	111
Input 2	9	3	1	0	93
Input 3	9	9	0	0	90
Input 4	1	9	1	3	36

Figure 6.2: C&E Matrix

Follow these steps to create a C&E matrix:

Step 1: Identify the outputs

Typically, the outputs are the customer requirements. As mentioned in Chapter 1, knowing and truly understanding your customers is the foundation of all these tools. This matrix is no exception. It doesn't make any sense to use it if you don't know what your manager or your stakeholders expect from you, or if you don't know what you are trying to accomplish. You must clearly define your goals. In this first step, list the requirements of your customers at the top of the matrix, across the columns. Ideally, do not list more than four to six requirements.

Step 2: Add weight

Rank the customer requirements by importance, using the following scale: 1 for low importance, 3 for moderate importance, and 9 for high importance. Keep in mind that they can't all be 1s or 9s. If most of your customer requirements are of low importance for example, either you didn't identify them correctly or the work you are about to perform is meaningless and qualifies as non-value added—in other words, busy work.

Step 3: List inputs

If you created a process flow, grab the steps from that tool and list them in the first column. If you want to prioritize your work, use the tasks from your to-do list. If you identified the potential causes of a problem using a Fishbone (see Chapter 5), but are not sure which ones to work on, consider the potential causes in the Fishbone as your inputs.

Step 4: Correlate the inputs to the outputs

In this step, you analyze and quantify the relationship between each listed input and each output, using the following scale: 9 for a strong cause-effect relationship, 3 for a moderate relationship, 1 for a weak relationship, and 0 for no relationship. For each matrix row-column intersection, ask yourself how strong is the effect of input 1 on each of the outputs. Then move to input 2, and so on, until you have placed the appropriate scores in all the matrix cells.

Step 5: Calculate weighted correlations

After you complete the matrix, calculate the weighted score for each row. Multiply the first matrix cell score by the weight of the first column, multiply the second cell score by the weight of the second column and repeat for each column in the row. Add the result from each column, for the entire row and place the number in the last column of the matrix. Then repeat the calculation in the other rows.

Step 6: Sort the matrix and apply the Pareto principle

Sort the matrix by the Total column from high to low, so the rows with high scores are at the top. The inputs in the rows with the highest values are most likely to have the largest impact on your outputs, and therefore on your customers.

Using the Pareto principle, which you will learn later in this chapter, identify the 20% that will have the greatest impact and focus on them first. They will produce 80% of the results. You should not, however, completely ignore the factors that scored lower. Even though they may not be as important to the customer, they may still have value and should be addressed at some point.

C&E Matrix EXAMPLE

In this example, coffee shop managers learned the requirements of their customers and what is most important to them. Customers would like the coffee to be hot and strong and they want it to be served fast while paying a low price. The type coffee brewing machine scored the highest and therefore is the most essential element to satisfy the customers.

There is a high correlation between the coffee machine and the temperature of the coffee. The water quality, on the flip side, is not that important. Do you think that investing in a state-of-the-art water purification system would improve customer satisfaction? It won't, because water quality had almost no correlation with customer requirements. However, the coffee shop may have to increase prices to recuperate the investment, which in fact could decrease customer satisfaction.

Cause & Effect Matrix

Importance to Customer →	9	9	3	1	Total
Customer Requirements (Outputs) →	Hot	Strong	Low Price	Fast Service	
Inputs ↓	Correlation of Input to Output				
Coffee machine	9	9	3	3	174
Coffee beans	0	9	9	0	108
Roast type	0	9	1	0	84
Coffee cup	9	0	3	1	91
Water	0	0	3	0	9

Figure 6.3: C&E Matrix Example

The Pareto Principle

You may have heard about this principle, but since you will be using it in step 6 of the C&E Matrix, here is a quick refresher.

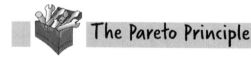

In 1906, an Italian economist, Vilfredo Pareto, created a mathematical formula to describe the distribution of wealth in his country. He realized that twenty percent of the people owned eighty percent of the wealth. In the 1940s, Dr. Joseph M. Juran recognized a universal principle he called the "vital few and trivial many" and attributed it to Pareto. It became known as the Pareto Principle, or the 80/20 Rule. According to this principle, 20 percent of resources are responsible for 80 percent of results.

So, what does this mean for you? For Pareto, it meant that 20 percent of the people owned 80 percent of the wealth. Juran's principle identified that 20 percent of the defects are causing 80 percent of the problems.

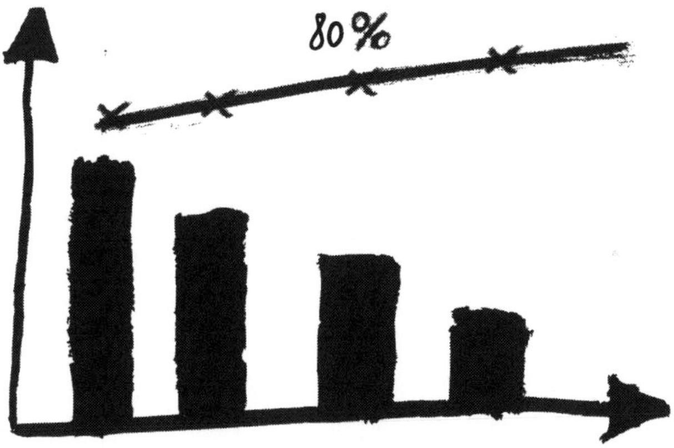

You can apply the 80/20 Rule to almost anything, from the science of management to the physical world. In your case, it is important to understand that 80 percent of your outcomes will come from 20 percent of your efforts. The challenge is to identify the most important factors and to focus on them. The C&E Matrix can help you with that.

Once you understand the Pareto Principle, you can apply it to many scenarios at different levels. For example, 80 percent of the sales of your organization come from 20 percent of your customers. This is another reason why you must know and understand your customers. You need to know who they are, what they want and then offer it to them. Most of your energy should be spent on the 20 percent.

In their book *The One Thing*, Gary Keller and Jay Papasan encourage us to take this principle even further and take 20 percent of the 20 percent of the 20 percent, and so on until you get to the most important thing to work on. They call this the "Extreme Pareto." You can start with a large list but, as they suggest, don't stop until you get to the critical few and then keep going until you get to the essential one. Working on the right thing versus wrong thing is the difference between being productive or just active, being effective or just efficient, and the only way to have more free time is doing less and getting better results.

"The key is to work out the few things that are really important, and the few methods that will give us what we really want."

–Richard Koch

7. IF ANYTHING CAN GO WRONG, FIX IT

"Intellectuals solve problems, geniuses prevent them."

– Albert Einstein

ANTICIPATE EVIL

According to Murphy's Law, anything that can go wrong will go wrong. This doesn't mean that you just have to wait around for things to go wrong. Being proactive and thinking of what could potentially be wrong with a product, a new process, or any improvement, is crucial. Often there are many things that could be wrong with a process or product, so it is helpful to analyze each step of the process or each critical component of the product to narrow the possibilities.

Identifying what could potentially go wrong allows you to address issues proactively and put proper controls in place to prevent them from happening. Or, in a worse-case scenario, if something goes wrong, it allows you to be prepared to fix it as soon as possible, hopefully with minimal or no customer impact. Remember, it is all about serving your customers and anticipating their needs. Anticipating the problems they may have with the service or your product can transform a satisfied customer into a delighted customer.

FMEA

Failure Modes and Effects Analysis (FMEA) is a detailed approach for identifying all potential failures in a design, process, product, or service. FMEA was originally developed by the U.S. Department of Defense in the 1940's as a systems engineering tool, but today it is widely used in many industries. Even though it was originally used in product development, it has also proved to be helpful in many areas of process improvement, especially when improving business processes or systems.

While the FMEA is a complex tool that may seem overwhelming at first, it is also one of the most powerful. If you understand how it works and how it can help, you will be able to use it in many situations.

This tool works best when done within teams of knowledgeable subject matter experts because you really have to understand each step of the process or product component before identifying what could go wrong. When using this tool, you start by looking at proposed solutions in detail, and then you identify all the potential failure areas.

FAILURE IS NOT AN OPTION

In short, **failure modes** are the ways in which a process or product can fail. **Effects** are the ways these failures can lead to defects and become waste. The FMEA is designed to identify, prioritize, and limit these failure modes. The sooner you discover a failure, the less it will cost to fix it, and the less severe the implications.

The FMEA can help you identify what could go wrong at early stages of process or product design, so that you can avoid severe consequences and a negative experience for the customers.

Think of the high-profile product recalls in recent years due to poorly designed products. It's not hard to come up with some examples if you've been following the news. Who is to blame? The blame usually falls on manufacturers for not providing a safe product, especially in the auto industry.

> "An ounce of prevention is worth a pound of cure."
>
> –Benjamin Franklin

There are many situations when you may choose to perform a FMEA:

1. When you are implementing a new process or improving an existing process

Improving a process is a good thing, but it also means changing the way things are done. Change comes with risks and the potential for failure, and the FMEA can help you mitigate those risks.

2. When you are creating a new product

A product doesn't have to be a complex machine or a new application for a smart phone. It could be as simple as a report that you are creating for your department or a presentation that you are preparing for your stakeholders.

3. When you are facing many specific problems

In this scenario, you need to understand which problems are the most critical, those that must be addressed first. For some of them you may have solid documentation and controls in place, but others can be exposed to various risks.

I encourage you to use this tool throughout the lifetime of a process or project because you should always be aiming for optimal results with minimal waste. When used properly, the FMEA offers substantial benefits by identifying errors in the very early stages of the design, production, or process.

The benefits of FMEA are more reliable products, less customer support required after sale, increased customer satisfaction, improved brand recognition, and lower warranty costs.

Process/ Process Step	Potential Failure Mode	Potential Failure Effects	S E V	Potential Causes	O C C	Current Controls	D E T	R P N	Recommended Actions
What is the process or step?	What could go wrong?	What is the effect on customer/ company?		What could cause the failure?		What controls are in place to prevent failures?			What are the actions for reducing the occurrence of the cause or improving detection?

SEV	**Severity** How severe is the effect on the customers? (10=most severe, 1=least severe)
OCC	**Occurrence** How often does the cause of failure mode occur? (10=highest occurrence, 1=lowest occurrence)
DET	**Detection** How well can you detect the cause or failure mode using current controls? (10=most difficult to detect, 1=easy to detect)
RPN	**Risk Priority Number** What is the risk related to the effects, causes, and controls? RPN=SEV x OCC x DET

Figure 7.1: FMEA

Follow these steps to build a FMEA:

Step 1: Assemble a cross-functional team of subject matter experts (SMEs) from different functional areas

You need as much knowledge as possible about the process, product, or service, and of course about your customers and their needs. A cross-functional approach is a must. I recommend that you don't even attempt using this tool alone. It's almost impossible to fill it out with accurate information on your own.

Step 2: Identify the scope and boundaries of the FMEA

If you created a project charter or a SIPOC, you can borrow them from there. While this may seem trivial, this step is important because it keeps you and your team focused.

Once you have your team identified and the scope clarified, start filling out the tool.

Step 3: Identify the key process steps/inputs or product components and list them in the first column

Copy them from other tools that you used for your project, such as the process map and the Fishbone, or use the ones that you prioritized in the C&E Matrix.

Step 4: For each of the elements identified in step 3, brainstorm all the ways a failure could happen

Ask what could possibly go wrong with each of the steps. These are the potential failure modes.

Step 5: Determine the effects of each failure on the outputs or on the customer

Identify the consequences that a potential failure can have on the system, department, organization, product, or customers.

Step 6: Determine the severity rating

Rate severity using a scale from 1 to 10, where 1 is low or no effect (least severe) and 10 is catastrophic (most severe). This shows how serious each effect is on the output or on the customer.

Step 7: Brainstorm potential causes

Use root cause analysis tools like the Fishbone or the Five Whys to get to the root cause faster. This is where the experience of the team can help you as well. Once you have identified the potential causes, list them here.

Step 8: For each cause, estimate and list the probability of the occurrence

Use a scale from 1 to 10, where 1 is low occurrence or extremely unlikely to occur, and 10 is inevitable. How often is the cause likely to occur and result in a failure mode?

Step 9: For each cause, identify and list the current process controls that are in place to prevent failure from reaching the customers

List controls such as tests, audits, or procedures. Ideally, they are able to prevent the causes from happening or at least reduce the likelihood of happening.

Step 10: Determine and list the detection rating for each control

Use a scale from 1 to 10, where 1 is easily detected and 10 means that either the control will not be able to detect the problem or that it is non-existent.

In most places that I have worked, the controls were non-existent or extremely ineffective; so make sure that you review each control and understand its effectiveness. Having procedures in place that haven't been updated in many years or tests that are not performed properly will result in a low score.

Step 11: Calculate the risk priority number (RPN)

Multiply the severity by the occurrence and detection scores. This number provides guidance to rank potential causes in the order you should be addressing them.

Step 12: Identify recommended actions

Review the items with the highest RPN and determine remediations. These recommended actions can be additional controls to improve detection, but this could also mean going back to the drawing board and reassessing a new process or identifying improvements. If you identify potential failures where you can't implement controls to prevent them, you may want to change your approach. Once you identify specific actions, I highly recommend that you assign someone to take ownership for completing each task, and that you set a target completion date.

Though this technique may be time-consuming because it involves various stakeholders, when it is implemented proactively it will be paramount to a successful completion of any project.

Keep in mind that while the FMEA can help you review the design of a process or product by assessing its risk of failure, it is not a substitute for good planning and engineering.

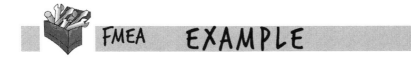

FMEA EXAMPLE

In the example below, the highest risk is the incomplete information captured from customers in the call center.

Failure Modes and Effects Analysis (FMEA)

	Process	Potential Failure Mode	Potential Failure Effects	SEV	Potential Causes	OCC	Current Controls	DET	RPN	Recommended Actions
	What is the process or process step?	*What could go wrong?*	*What is the effect on the customer or company?*		*What could cause the failure?*		*What controls are in place to prevent failures?*			*What are the actions for reducing the occurrence of the cause or improving detection?*
1	Call centers	Incomplete information captured from customers	Non-billable transactions	6	Agents not capturing all the information from customers	8	Training	10	**480**	Make fields mandatory in the front end system
2	Billing	Incomplete invoices sent to clients	Missed revenue	9	Analysts forget to include manual transactions	2	SOP, training	7	**126**	Review/update SOPs Quarterly training sessions
3	Billing	Invoices submitted late	Missed revenue	9	System not identifying all billable transactions	5	Audit process	2	**90**	Review/update audit process including documentation

Figure 7.2: FMEA Example

In this example, even though the severity for item 1 is not as high as the other two items, the risk factor (RPN) is the highest. The RPN can be higher for a lower-severity item when there are no controls in place to prevent it from happening. Training alone is not really a reliable control. The best control is to make the required information fields mandatory in the system so this will force the agents to capture all the information. This will prevent the failure.

Consider the flip side. In line 3 of the example, the audit process is considered a more robust control that has the potential to catch the transactions that were not identified by the system. Even though the RPN is much lower, there is still an opportunity for reviewing and updating the audit process—or implementing additional controls—since the failure still happens occasionally.

"Planning is bringing the future into the present so that you can do something about it now."

-Alan Lakein

You have now learned how to implement the FMEA tool to provide an objective analysis and to create a plan to address potential issues in your process or product.

Congratulations! You have learned the analysis tools and now we will review the tools to implement, communicate, and sustain the results.

8. IMPLEMENT LIKE A PRO

"Ideas are useless unless used. The proof of their value is in their implementation. Until then, they are in limbo."

– Theodore Levitt

SHOW RESULTS

Now that you have identified the root causes of problems and have brainstormed improvements, you should coordinate their implementation. If your title is not project manager and you don't have a PMP certification, don't worry. Most likely you will not have to manage complex projects with large budgets, but you still need basic skills to keep the project on track and to ensure that the improvements you proposed will actually happen.

Don't overlook the implementation because no matter how much effort you put into identifying problems using the process improvement tools, you will ultimately be evaluated by your outcomes. Your managers will not care about the tools or the methodologies you use—they only care about the results.

To make an impact, you must implement your improvements; more often than not, you will interact with cross-functional teams and persuade people to help you achieve the desired results. You must, however, have a plan and be organized to keep everyone focused so that you hit the target dates.

Project management is like juggling many balls at once—you have to keep your eyes on all of them and catch each one at the right time. If you don't, the show is ruined. The balls are the activities that you have to control so they get completed on time. Missing a deadline on a task could have significant effects on the rest of the project.

That's why it is crucial to be able to identify and understand everything that needs to get done and to know when each activity has to be completed.

Gantt Chart

One of the most popular project management tools is the Gantt Chart, which was developed in the early 1900s by an engineer named Henry Gantt. He designed this tool to help manufacturing supervisors track the work and understand if it was on time, ahead of, or behind schedule. This is the foundation of the chart being used today by many project managers across all industries.

Gantt charts offers a great visual snapshot of an entire project—the tasks that need to be performed, in what order, and when they have to be finished. When you first set up a chart, you need to consider all the actions that will be involved in your project, who can help you with each task, how long each task will take, and what are the dependencies between tasks.

It is also helpful to think what could potentially go wrong, and ideally prepare some workarounds in case you encounter any problems. You will often hear the term "critical path." This refers to the sequence of tasks that must be completed individually so the entire project can be delivered on time.

"A project without a critical path is like a ship without a rudder."

-D. Meyer

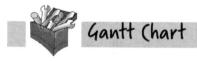

The Gantt chart is also a powerful tool to communicate the progress to your stakeholders and to show the implications of missed deadlines or schedule changes. It is a useful tool for planning and scheduling your projects, for assessing the duration of the project, and for identifying the resources needed.

How to Create a Gantt Chart

There are many project management programs that you can use to create a Gantt chart. Microsoft Project is one of the most popular, but you can also use Excel templates that you can find for free online. It's easy to be tempted by the dozens of expensive programs, but you don't really need them. You can even draw one by hand if you understand how it works.

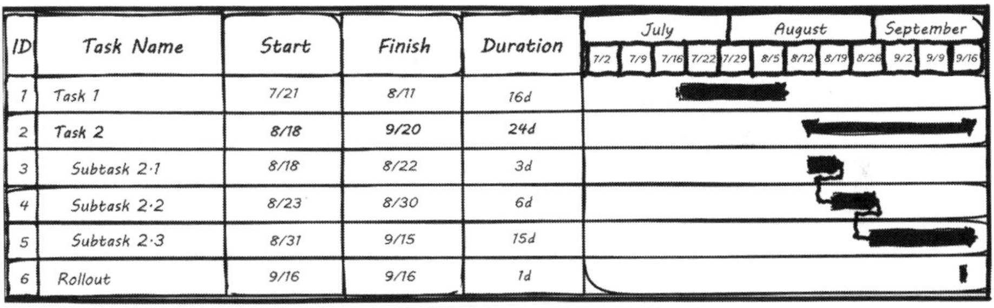

ID
Task Name
Start
Finish
Duration
July
August
September
7/2 7/9 7/16 7/22 7/29 8/5 8/12 8/19 8/26 9/2 9/9 9/16
1 Task 1 7/21 8/11 16d
2 Task 2 8/18 9/20 24d
3 Subtask 2·1 8/18 8/22 3d
4 Subtask 2·2 8/23 8/30 6d
5 Subtask 2·3 8/31 9/15 15d
6 Rollout 9/16 9/16 1d

Figure 8.1: Gantt Chart

Follow these steps to create a Gantt Chart:

Step 1: Identify the objective

List the improvements you are about to implement. Be specific when defining the scope. As we learned in Chapter 2 when we covered the project charter, defining the scope and objective of a project is a critical step before beginning the project.

Step 2: Identify the essential tasks

List all the activities that have to be performed. If you don't include all the tasks that need to take place, the tool becomes useless. In project management, there is a tool called WBS (Work Breakdown Structure) that helps organize the work into more manageable sections. If you feel like your project is too big and that there are too many tasks to be performed, this will help you. For example, if your project involves multiple departments, you can separately identify the tasks that have to be performed by IT, Marketing, and Finance. Then you can combine them or you can manage them separately.

Step 3: For each of the tasks identified in step 2, note the starting date and the estimated duration

Make sure that you consult the people who perform the tasks before recording any dates in your plan.

Step 4: Identify the relationships between tasks

Some tasks can't begin before the previous one has ended. For example, if you want to implement a standardized process, you can't implement it until you design it. These types of tasks are called linear tasks, while tasks that can be done at the same time are called parallel tasks.

The reason it is important to classify the tasks is to be able to note the relationships between the sequential tasks. Once you capture the relationships, you will have a deeper understanding of how to organize your project and to schedule activities on the chart.

Understanding dependencies is critical in project management. In Gantt charts, there are three main relationships between linear tasks:

Finish to Start – tasks that can't start before a previous and related task is completed.

Start to Start – tasks that can't start until a preceding task starts.

Finish to Finish – tasks that can't end before a preceding task ends.

Step 5: Maintain the chart

As you start your implementation, your project will evolve and things will change. It's important to be organized and to update the chart with the changes as soon as they occur. This will help you stay in control of your project. Gantt Charts are great for monitoring the progress of the project, but the trick is to *act* as soon as you notice that the project has gotten behind schedule and bring it back on course.

I have only covered the very basics of a Gantt Chart in this book, because that I don't expect that you will be managing complex projects in your role unless you are a project manager. Gantt charts are useful, however, and I highly recommend that you read more about them and understand how to create them. There is plenty of free information available online on this topic.

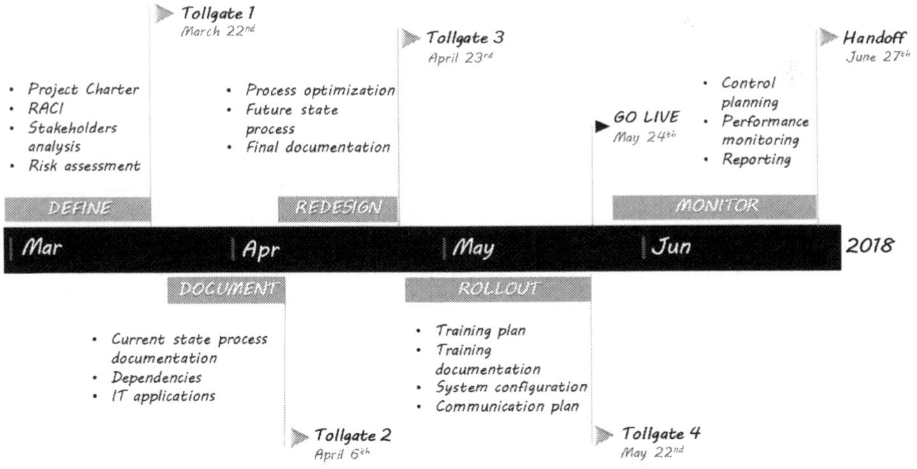

Figure 8.2: Sample Project Time Line

If you ever need to share a project plan with senior management, it helps to create a visual time line and only include the milestones of the project. They will not have the patience or the desire to review the project plan task by task. I created the time line in *Figure 8.2* using MS Power Point.

FORM SOLID PROJECT MANAGEMENT HABITS

If you are new to project management, the following tips will help you form habits that can dramatically improve the way you run your project team meetings.

1. Listen

Because it is your project and you are the lead, you may feel like you have to do all the talking in meetings, barely allowing the other participants to get a word in. You may want to get your point across and make sure that everyone understands that you are in charge. In reality, even if you *are* the lead of the project, you are probably not a subject matter expert on many topics. You rely on cross-functional participation to implement your improvements. Listen to what others have to say. If you ask a question, wait for the answer; don't jump in with other questions at the same time.

2. Always create a meeting agenda and send meeting notes

Sending a meeting agenda before the meeting serves at least two purposes. First, it helps people understand what will be discussed at the meeting so they can decide if they must be present. Second, it helps you stay on track and manage your time during the meeting so you are able to cover everything. Without an agenda, people may come unprepared. It will be extremely difficult to stay on track and cover everything, especially if the meeting is only one hour long. The more you can clarify expectations, the more people are likely to come to the meeting and engage with you.

If you don't summarize the take-aways in an email shortly after the meeting, you have wasted everyone's time—especially if you agreed on action items during the meeting. I don't think anybody really enjoys sending out meeting minutes, but taking a few minutes to summarize the discussion in a few bullet points helps everyone.

3. Know your customers

Always keep in mind who your customers are, both internal and external. Never lose sight of their needs, requirements, or expectations. By doing so, if at any time the project gets off track or if you are unsure which direction to go, asking yourself what your customers want or what you are trying to ultimately deliver for the customers can help you and your team get back on track.

4. Be flexible

No matter how clear the objective and the scope, how organized you are, and how hard you keep everyone focused by following a strict agenda, things change. As you learn more about different processes and as you interact with more people, you may get or hear ideas that never crossed your mind at the beginning of the project.

If you are rigid, seeing things only in black or white with no gray in between, you will miss great opportunities. Keep your eyes open; be flexible and adaptable. Sometimes you must even be ready to improvise. Be the person who is ready for change and always armed with sound approaches for unexpected situations. Don't think that being inflexible is a sign of being in charge. In fact, the opposite is true. Sometimes the person with the most flexibility—not the most power—is in control.

5. Be honest and fair

Most of the time, especially during an implementation project, you will rely on help from people who don't report to you. Sometimes you may even have to persuade them to drop what they are doing to help you. And by persuasion I don't mean manipulation. While manipulation forces someone to do something that is not in their own interest, persuasion means getting people to do things that benefit you and are also in their own best interest.

It is almost impossible to persuade someone who is not interested in what you are doing. Since we are all interested in ourselves, the best way to get someone interested is to talk about them and make sure they understand what's in it for them. Being honest and fair and treating people as you like to be treated certainly helps. It is okay to create a sense of urgency and to hold people accountable to deadlines that are agreed on, but the way you do it makes a huge difference. Make people feel appreciated and be thankful for the help you get from them. Don't make them feel like they owe you anything.

"Leadership is the art of getting someone else to do something you want done because he wants to do it."

—Dwight D. Eisenhower

KEEP IT UNDER CONTROL

After the improvements are implemented, while you get a sense of accomplishment and some recognition from your peers and your manager, don't get too excited. Your job is not quite done yet. The question is, how do you make sure that all the changes will stay in place? Who will be responsible and accountable for making sure that people do not revert to what they were doing before? What will be the action if the process does go out of spec?

A control plan can help you answer these questions and many others related to the sustainability of the changes you made.

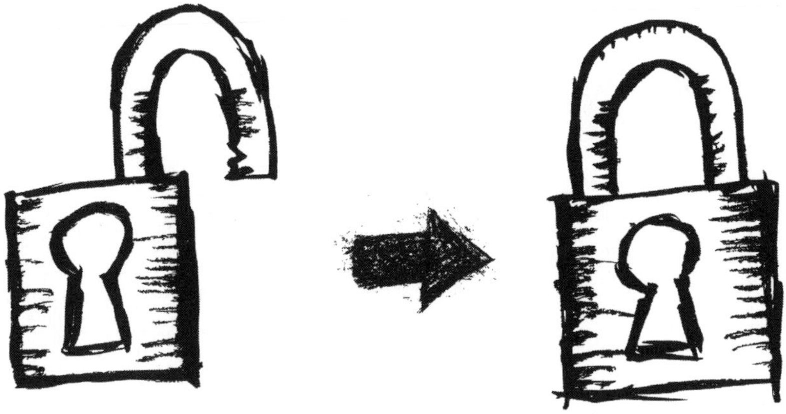

Control Plan

Even though a control plan is a simple tool, it often gets ignored because project leads, after everything is implemented, often feel that it is not their job any longer to monitor progress.

I encourage you to create a control plan for your projects because if you don't, you take a risk that all that hard work you put into making a difference could turn out to be a waste of time.

Process Step	Requirement	Specification		Measurement Method	Frequency
		USL	LSL		
Enter process step	What is the requirement?	Enter USL	Enter LSL	What is the performance measure?	How often do you check?

Who	Where Recorded	Corrective Action	SOP Reference
Who is responsible?	Where is the audit being recorded?	What action needs to be taken to rectify issue?	What documentation should be consulted?

Figure 8.3: The Key Elements of a Control Plan

Below are the key elements of a control plan. Feel free to add to it to capture additional information.

1. Process step

In this column you will list the steps in the improved process that are critical and should become control points. If anything fails during a step, the entire process will be compromised. I found that the easiest way to identify the control points is to review the process flow of the redesigned process.

2. Requirement

What is the requirement for each step so the process keeps running smoothly?

3. Specification

Here you will list the Upper Spec Limit (USL) and Lower Spec Limit (LSL) of the requirement. In some instances, you may only have one of them, an USL or a LSL, but not both.

4. Measurement Method

How will the data be collected and measured? Will someone collect a sample of data every month, or it can be obtained from a report?

5. Frequency

How often will this step be monitored? Daily, weekly, or monthly?

6. Who

While it is important to make sure that the task to monitor controls is assigned to a specific person, I recommend that you list the role of the person, not the name, since people constantly come and go.

7. Where recorded

It is helpful to create a log file where the people responsible for monitoring the control will keep track of the monitoring activities.

8. Corrective action

Be specific about the action that needs to be taken if the control goes out of spec so the responsible person knows exactly what to do. I suggest that you create a reaction plan for the responsible party to make it clear what steps must be followed to keep the process going with minimum disruptions.

9. SOP Reference

It goes without saying that you must properly document any changes you made to a process in a redesigned process flow and a standard operating procedure document (SOP). In this column, list the documentation that can be referenced in case the person monitoring the control has any questions about the new process.

For a control plan to work, you must ensure that you identify the process owner. Once you have implemented improvements and made changes to a process, the process owner is responsible for the management of the process going forward.

Typically, process owners are current leaders or managers of the organization, but often they hold non-leadership positions. A process owner should understand the process, must feel the pain of a broken process, and must appreciate the gains of the improved process. You should partner with the process owner from the beginning of the project, stay in close contact for the duration of the project, and keep in touch for at least a couple of months after project completion for additional support.

In fact, the process owner plays such an important role in a Six Sigma project, that I don't usually begin working on a process improvement project without proper ownership. The process owner becomes one of my top customers.

Once you complete the control plan, make sure to review it in detail with all the stakeholders and departments mentioned in the control plan, including the process owner.

Control Plan EXAMPLE

In the example illustrated in *Figure 8.4*, one of the control points in the new process of processing claims is to review a transaction backlog. The requirement is to have minimal active transactions on the backlog, and I set the upper limit (USL) at 5—which means that no action is necessary until there are five transactions in the log. The measurement is done by simply reviewing the monthly report from FP&A (Financial Planning and Analysis), and this action is performed by the Director of Operations, who will record the audit in an Excel spreadsheet located on the L: Drive.

If there are more than five transactions in the log, he will follow up immediately with the Claims department to address the issue, and if there are questions about the process, the SOP XYZ-234 contains the detailed process and instructions on how to handle exceptions.

Add other steps and control points as applicable, following the same logic described above.

Control Plan

Step	Requirement	Specification		Measurement Method	Frequency
		USL	LSL		
Reviewing backlog	No transactions at end of month	5	0	Report from FP&A	Monthly

Who	Where Recorded	Corrective Action	SOP Reference
Director of Ops.	Excel file on L: drive	Follow up with Claims	XYZ-234

Figure 8.4: Control Plan Example

9. PRESENT SO PEOPLE WILL LISTEN

"The audience are likely to remember only three things from your presentation or speech."

– Stephen Keague

CAPTIVATE YOUR AUDIENCE

From time to time, you may have to share your project findings, presenting your ideas or suggestions for improvement, and this means that you will have to stand in front of people. I am sure that few people love giving presentations and speaking in front of groups. For many it can be terrifying, even if you do it often. You may be nervous and you may be shaking in your boots, perhaps even losing sleep the night before. Don't worry. You are not alone.

Everybody gets nervous speaking in front of people, and this includes professional actors and even experienced public speakers invited to give TED talks. While it is true that the more you do it, the better and more confident you get, your nerves will never go away completely. In fact, shaking knees and sweaty palms are a good indication that you actually care about your presentation and your audience. So, there is nothing wrong with being nervous. Just welcome the feeling and accept it.

I decided to include a chapter about presentations after I attended a painful presentation during a quarterly meeting. The material was good and informative, but it was so boring that it almost put the eighty-person audience into a deep sleep—needless to say, the presentation was after a pasta and meatballs lunch.

If you don't take the time to properly craft the presentation with the audience in mind, you are wasting everyone's time—even if you do an excellent job delivering it. Both content and delivery are equally important.

My goal is to give you a few tips on how to captivate your audience —how to present so people will actually listen. But before you deliver the presentation, you obviously have to prepare the content and rehearse the delivery.

PREPARE WELL

Step 1: Identify the purpose of your presentation

There are many reasons for giving a presentation: for training, to give a status update on a project, to present the findings of research, or to gain alignment on proposed improvements. Depending on the purpose of your presentation, you must clearly identify what you want the audience to take away from the presentation and what your goals are. Are you seeking approval? If so, bear in mind that you are selling something; you are selling your ideas, and your goal is to convince the audience to buy into them.

Step 2: Know your audience

Now that you have defined the purpose of the presentation, it is time to focus on your audience. As I mentioned in Chapter 1, you must be aware of who your customers are and get to know them as well as you can. This also holds true for your audience.

Learning as much as you can about your audience is the very first step. Don't even attempt to create a slide deck before answering a few basic questions: Who is your audience? How much do they know about the subject? How big will your audience be? What level of the organization will you be speaking to? Are you presenting to a senior leadership team or middle management? Knowing these answers will help you create a targeted presentation and prepare for delivery.

Step 3: Structure your presentation

Think of your presentation like a story with a beginning, middle and end. First you have to draw your audience in with a catchy introduction. I know that many people like to start with a summary of the presentation—this is what I am going to talk about in the first part, then I will talk about something else, and I will wrap up with a conclusion.

I am not a big fan of the agenda slide. I like presentations to be unfolding stories, and I find these agenda slides to be like movie spoilers. Imagine going to a movie and in the first few minutes you see a summary of the plot. How engaged are you going to be from that point on? There will be no tension at all; you might as well get up and leave.

Another way of starting a presentation is to set the expectations for the audience so that by the end of the presentation, they will learn X, or they will be required to do Y. A critical point to remember: do not start creating the slides before you define the story you want to tell.

Step 4: Create your slides

I don't think anybody is a big fan of Power Point slides, but like them or not, they remain still the most commonly used vehicle for delivering presentations. When you hear the word *slides*, you probably think of boring, busy slides that someone is reading in front of a group of people. That doesn't have to be the case.

Once you have identified the audience and have drafted the story you want to tell, it is time to create the slides. I always ask how much time I have for my presentation, not how many slides I should have. I would much rather have ten attractive and easy-to- follow slides than four slides loaded with information and charts that will guarantee to immediately lose the audience.

The more information you have on one slide, the more likely your audience will focus on the screen and tune out what you are saying, especially if you use bullet points. You will also be tempted to read from your slide and turn your back to your audience.

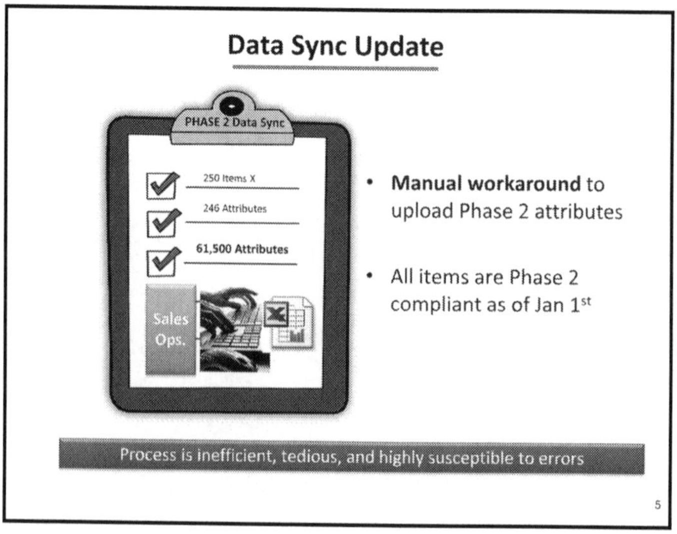

Figure 9.1: Example Slide

Have a look at the slide in *Figure 9.1*. Part of the talk can be something like this: "Phase 2 data sync is complete and compliant as of January first. The process, however, is inefficient and susceptible to errors because a tremendous amount of data is being entered manually by Sales Operations into an Excel spreadsheet". The slide contains a lot of information and numbers and yet is not overwhelming or difficult to follow.

I do prefer using images in my slides. A picture is definitely worth a thousand words when it comes to your presentation because powerful images can amplify what you say. It's okay to have a few words in short sentences on each slide, as long as the font is big enough so people can read them. As a rule of thumb, if it can't be read, it doesn't belong on the slide.

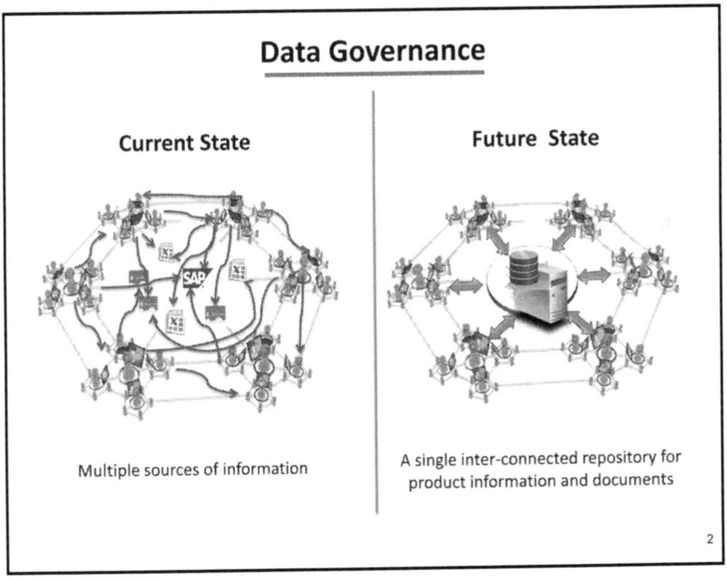

Figure 9.2: Use of Images Example

Animations can be tempting, and you may think it is cool to have slides spinning and words rotating, but it can be extremely distracting to the audience. Use animations sparingly.

Step 5: Rehearse the presentation

If you assume that you know the material and there is no need to rehearse, you are wrong; when you find yourself in front of the audience, you will immediately start to read the slides, and if something happens to the projector or the remote, you will start to panic and you will be lost.

I suggest that you practice your presentation out loud, just as if you are delivering the talk. This is a good opportunity to time yourself to ensure that you will be able to complete it in the allotted time.

I often hear people asking how long a presentation should be. Thankfully, there is an answer backed by neuroscience and powerful real-world evidence. The answer is 18 minutes. According to TED Talks curator Chris Anderson, 18 minutes is "short enough to hold people's attention, including on the Internet, and precise enough to be taken seriously. But it is also long enough to say something that matters."

When you practice, it helps if you record and listen to yourself or have a friend or a family member listen to your presentation and give you feedback.

Step 6: Anticipate

If something can go wrong, it will go wrong, but you must be prepared to handle it. What if the projector stops working? Do you have paper copies available? This is where step 5 really helps. Even if you are not able to project and didn't make paper copies, if you rehearsed, you should know your material extremely well. In this case you should have no problems delivering your presentation.

Anticipating the audience's reaction to certain topics or slides and potential questions is not easy, but I encourage you to at least attempt doing it. If you practice in front of a friend or family member, you can also get some ideas on how the audience may react. This way you can prepare and have most answers ready so they will roll of the tip of your tongue.

Step 7: Visit the room before the presentation

Knowing the room helps more than you think. If you are not familiar with it, make sure to check it out at least one day before the presentation. This helps you plan where you will be standing or sitting, decide if you need a microphone, and assess whether the room is large enough for your audience.

If you are the meeting organizer, check to see if your meeting invite was forwarded to other people. If so, are there enough chairs in the room? If you are about to present in a conference room, try booking the room at least half an hour in advance to have time to get everything set up. There is nothing worse than having a bunch of people watching you set up a non-responsive projector, trying to connect to Skype, or opening a phone bridge for the people who will be attending remotely.

I know this all sounds like common sense, but I am sure you have attended meetings where the organizer's lack of preparation is blamed on "technical difficulties." Do not skip this step.

"During the first few minutes of your presentation, your job is to assure the audience members that you are not going to waste their time and attention."

–Dale Ludwig

DELIVER FLAWLESSLY

1. Break up the tension

No matter how much you prepare, you will be nervous and you will notice any tension in the room, especially if the audience doesn't know who you are. The best way to break the tension is to get a quick laugh, which not only lightens the mood, but also helps you relax a bit. You can start with a quick joke, but if you have to work too hard to come up with one, it's probably not a good idea.

"The best way to make your audience laugh is to start laughing yourself."

-Oliver Goldsmith

Another option is to start with a Steve Jobs line, something like "So, I've been waiting for this moment for a long time." This helps bring the audience to your side, since they will sense you are going to tell a story.

2. Be aware of your voice

Studies have shown that we tend to tune out a high-pitched, shrill voice, and pay more attention to deep, fuller voices because they exude confidence and authority. The problem is that when we are nervous, all the tension in our bodies is reflected in our voices. And that is because we are not breathing deeply, which makes our voice sound shallow and high. The best way to fix this is to breathe and to pay attention to the timbre of your voice. It also helps to vary the pitch of your voice; otherwise the presentation will be monotonous and boring.

3. Slow down

When we are uncomfortable, we tend to speed up because we want to get through the presentation as fast as possible. We want to get it done quickly and we want to make sure we get through all the slides. Unfortunately, this will impact the clarity and the quality of your presentation. If you practice your presentation aloud, you should know how long it will take, so there is no reason to rush through it.

4. Do not read the slides

I see this happening all the time—people just reading the screen with their back at the audience. That's an absolute big NO. First of all, you should never turn your body away from the audience; that's the moment you will lose the connection. Second, if you start reading your slides, it means that you didn't prepare enough. You should know your content by heart.

5. Do not pace around

Pacing around can be very distracting to the audience. I suggest that you stand still, with your feet shoulder-width apart toward the audience and your arms on the side of your body. Do not cross your arms and do not place your hands in your pockets. I find it helpful to hold something in my hand. It could be the remote for the projector or a pen, but I make sure not to play with it while speaking because that can also be very distracting. This also applies if you sit at the table. Do not cross your arms. Make sure that your hands are visible at all times; do not keep them under the table.

6. Avoid uhms and ahs

Filler words are common in presentations and they are so annoying. The best way to find out if you use uhms and ahs is to have someone give you feedback. The easiest way to stop this is to use a quick pause instead. That's also a perfect time to remember to take a quick breath. I am sure you've attended meetings when the presenter kept talking and talking without stopping or breathing as if there were no commas or periods in the sentences.

7. Stay in the moment

Take a deep breath, be yourself, and picture your audience naked. You've probably heard this advice before. If you really want to picture someone naked, picture yourself, not the audience. You need to be vulnerable and be yourself. I tried once picturing the audience naked and it freaked me out so badly that I hardly remembered what I wanted to say. Don't even try it. Concentrate on the message, not on the way you feel. Anyway, it's not about you, it's about your audience.

Unexpected things happen from time to time. An audience member drops something, a phone with a funny ring tone breaks the silence, or construction work can be going on full blast on the floor above you. Do not ignore it. It's better to acknowledge it and make a joke if appropriate, because if you don't, it will be very disruptive to the audience. Never be mean about it and never insult anybody.

I was giving a presentation once and an audience member in the front row stepped out halfway through the presentation, probably to use the bathroom. A couple of seconds after she left, her phone started ringing in her pocketbook, and of course everyone was annoyed. I immediately thought that ignoring it was not an option since it was so loud, so I started polling the audience to see if they knew what song and artist it was. We had fun with that for a few minutes, until the woman came back and confirmed that our guesses were incorrect. But who cares, we had a good time with it.

8. Smile and make eye contact with the audience

Even though this may sound like common sense, many presenters fail to do it. By constantly making eye contact with different members of the audience, you will build a strong rapport with them. This helps the audience connect with you. You will also feel less nervous, because you will realize that you are talking to individuals, not a mass of people. And don't forget to smile while you are scanning the audience and maintaining great eye contact.

> "I always like to think I'm having a dinner party, and I'm the host, and the audience are my guests."
>
> –Caroline Rhea

9. Use the "B" key

Sometimes you may have to move off-topic for a short while, perhaps to tell a quick story. If you have an unrelated slide on the screen, you will not get the full attention of the audience, since most people will be focused on the slide shown. By pressing the "B" key of your laptop while your slide is showing, the screen will go blank, so that all the attention is on you. Hit the key again and the image reappears.

Keep in mind that with time, you will get better at speaking in front of people. The more you do it, the more you will improve. Toastmasters is a great opportunity to improve your public speaking skills. I strongly recommend looking for a club in your area.

10. WRITE EMAILS SO PEOPLE WILL READ THEM

"Clarity in business writing is not a luxury."

– Sir Richard Branson

NO MORE UNCLEAR EMAILS

Email overload is becoming an increasing issue in today's organizations. There are days when I get well over one hundred emails, and honestly, I ignore most of them. And that is not just because some of them are sent by people being overly polite or who hit *reply all* when they just mean to thank the sender for something. I am more frustrated with the long and boring emails that I don't even understand how to handle. Do I have to take any action, or is it just an FYI?

I always thought that every email we write is a reflection on us, our department and even our company. It's crucial for each email that leaves our outbox to be polished and professional.

Business emails are different from other forms of email. Any business email usually falls into one of the five categories below. The category must be clear to the reader, who should not have to spend a lot of time trying to make sense of it.

An email may serve different purposes, but the most common are to inform, to request, to record, to persuade, and to instruct.

1. To inform

We send this type of email when we want to inform people about the status of a project or to share information. When we covered the RACI Matrix in Chapter 2, you probably recall that some stakeholders only need to be informed (I). No action is expected from the recipients and it helps to make it clear by mentioning FYI in the subject line or in the first line of the email.

2. To request

The purpose of this type of email is to request something from the receiver(s). It could be information, data, a report, or even an answer to a question. Since you are expecting people to provide you something, it helps to mention something like *Action Requested* in the subject line or at the beginning of the email.

3. To record

Meeting minutes, for example, fall in this category. You just want to document the takeaways of a meeting or even a quick discussion that you had. No specific action is expected unless you misstated something and a recipient wants to add or clarify something.

4. To persuade

This is the most delicate type of email since you may want to influence someone that you don't have any authority over. If you are involved in a cross-functional initiative/project, you probably have to write this type of email often. You want to do everything that you can to get people on your side so they will help you achieve certain goals or objectives, even if they don't report to you and they are not obligated to help you.

5. To instruct

You typically send this type of email when you need to send specific

instruction on how to perform a specific task: how to run a report, how to handle a situation, etc.

Before your write an email, take a few minutes to identify its purpose. Always keep the readers in mind and remember that it's about them, not about you. Why do they need the information? What do you want them to take away from this communication? Do they need to take any action?

KNOW YOUR AUDIENCE

We learned in Chapter 1 about the importance of knowing your customer and in Chapter 9 about knowing your audience. The same principle applies to the emails you write. You must know or at least attempt to know your audience.

The key elements you need to know are:

1. To whom you are writing

First of all, it helps to know the gender of the recipient, since names can be confusing. It also helps to know the recipient's function and department.

2. The reader's knowledge

Based on the step above, you can gauge the knowledge of the audience. If you are writing about an IT matter to a finance audience, chances are that they will not be familiar with the topic and the terminology. In this case, be more specific and use common words so they can understand what you are talking about.

3. The reader's interest level

If readers have no interest in the topic, they may ignore it or delete it immediately. This is when the subject line and the first paragraph become extremely important. You must grab the attention of the reader immediately.

4. Why you are writing the message

Now that you are familiar with your audience, ask yourself why you are writing the message, and classify it in one of the five categories we covered earlier in this chapter.

Once you understand your audience and you know the type of email you are about to write, you can start identifying the key elements that you want to include. Leaving out critical details will confuse the reader and probably start a chain of reply emails asking for clarification. So, it is imperative to identify what should be included in the email and what should be left out because it is unnecessary.

Keep in mind that less is more when it comes to business emails. Be brief, but clear. If you believe that some information is unnecessary for the reader to understand the essence of the message, delete it.

"People who write obscurely are either unskilled in writing or up to mischief."

–Sir Peter Medawar

To avoid confusion, as a rule of thumb, try not to have more than two topics included in the same message—one topic is actually better—and no more than two or three key points per topic. Having too many topics or too many key points will overwhelm the reader, and will increase the risk of the message being ignored.

STRUCTURE AN EMAIL LIKE A STORY

Think of an email message like a story. It must have a beginning, a middle, and an end. A story also has paragraphs, which makes it much easier to read. The difference is that in an email you can get away with shorter paragraphs, as long as you don't sacrifice clarity for brevity. I often use one- or two-sentence paragraphs in emails because I find them easier to follow and less overwhelming.

In photography, the white space (or negative space) is the area that surrounds the subject of a photo. It plays an important role in the composition of a picture because it helps emphasize the subject by attracting the eye of the viewer. The same is true for emails and any other written material. The white space between the paragraphs is more important than you may think, because it helps lead the eye of the reader.

The **first paragraph** is the opening of the email. It must have at least two key elements: an attention grabber and a clear outline of the topic. This is the first thing that the reader sees. It can make or break your email. If you don't grab the reader from the very beginning and if you don't make clear what the message is about, you increase the chance of the viewer hitting the delete key before reading the email. The first paragraph is extremely important, since it sets the tone of the email.

The **middle of the message** adds more meat and provides more detail on the topic that you highlighted in the first paragraph. Here you provide numbers, facts, and expand on your topic. You may have multiple paragraphs in this section, but make sure to limit each of them to one topic. The opening of each paragraph must be strong enough to keep the reader's attention. If you arrange the information in a logical flow and if you focus on the readers, you increase the chance of bringing them in.

The **ending** summarizes your message and provides closing thoughts to wrap up your idea. The end section of your message also must restate the topic since the opening and the closing must always match. You can also include a call to action if you want the reader to take any action, but you must clearly ask for action. Never drop hints or imply things, even if you are afraid of being perceived as demanding

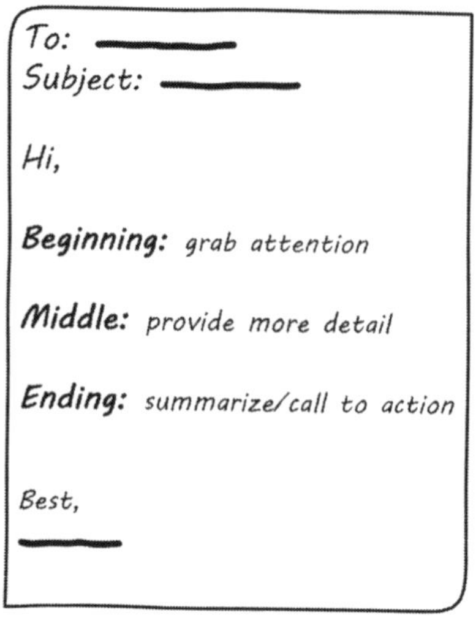

or of being turned down. Simply ask the reader to take a specific action by a specific date and time.

Transition words help link paragraphs together and help maintain the reader's attention. The most common transition words to express consequence are: *so*, *therefore*, and *as a result.* To summarize key points, you may use *in short* or *in conclusion. In other words* is used to restate something, and if you need to emphasize similarity you can use *in the same way* or *likewise.*

KEEP IT SIMPLE

To ensure that your emails do get read and that you get your point across, follow these suggestions:

1. Choose the appropriate greeting

Hi followed by the recipient's name is fine, but if you write to a group, avoid *Hi All*, since this is very impersonal. It's better to use the name of the group in place of *all* (Fin Ops, Marketing, Human Resources, etc.).

The closing is also important. *Best regards* or even *Thank you* are the safest—use the latter when you ask for something in return.

2. Use the active voice

This will make your email clearer and more direct. Using the passive voice in your business emails weakens the message you are communicating.

3. Use plain language and short sentences

Eliminate excess words. I encourage you to read your message multiple times. The more times you read the message, the higher the chances you will discover unnecessary words. Most of your sentences should follow the subject-verb-object format.

"Using plain English is not just a good intention. It is a business necessity."

-Lord Alexander of Weedon

4. Be aware of the tone

Even though vocal inflections are not present, your messages have a perceived tone; the wrong tone can be damaging to the business and personal relationships. DO NOT USE ALL CAPS, since this implies shouting and desperation.

5. Avoid acronyms and jargon

If you use acronyms, make sure to describe the meaning in parentheses. Jargon is terminology that relates to a specific industry, sport, etc. You should avoid words like *touch base*, *drill down*, *bandwidth*, or even worse, *at the end of the day*. These are jargon words that have become slang; not everybody will understand their meaning, especially if they are from different parts of the world.

6. Proofread, proofread, proofread

Typos make you appear unprofessional—you may get a pass (but only one!) if the language you are writing in is not your mother tongue. Proofreading is crucial before sending an email. To make sure that I don't mistakenly send an unfinished message, I never add the names of the recipients until I am finished editing the message.

YES, YOU CAN HELP!

7. Never say "no"

If you are the recipient of an email asking for your assistance and you are unable to help, list other options or point the sender in the right direction. I know this is common sense, but too often people will simply say "no" instead of being helpful. Saying "no" can damage business relationships, and for that reason I recommend that you talk about what you *can* do. In some instances, it is better to pick up the phone or walk over to the sender's desk and clarify the situation.

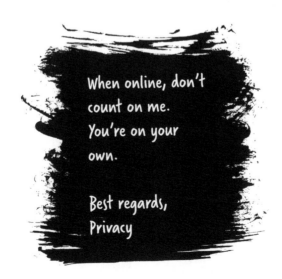

When online, don't count on me. You're on your own.

Best regards,
Privacy

A vital thing to keep in mind is that like anything else you do online, privacy is not guaranteed. Sometimes we wright message when we are frustrated or upset at someone, and our negative feelings make us write messages that we later regret. The best way to deal with this type of situation is to save the email as a draft and come back to it later, after the emotions have subsided and you can read it again with a clear mind.

"Before you press *Send*, always ask yourself, 'Would I be proud of this email if it were on the front page of the newspaper?' Because what is in writing can easily be shared with others," advises Jennifer Brown, founder and CEO of PeopleTactics.

And one more thing: remember to add the recipient name only after you make sure that your email is clear, to the point, and error-free.

CONGRATULATIONS!

If you made it this far, I trust that you want to make a difference. From this point on, you are distancing yourself from average; you are at war with mediocrity. You are tired of being a follower and you are ready to lead.

Have you noticed how, when entering a store, most people follow the person who previously entered the building? They use the exact same door, even though there are many other doors available and some of them are more accessible. Most people follow the path of a predecessor because it's much easier. Most people are either too shy to lead or they don't want to commit because it takes hard work and determination. But you are not like most people. You are different: you are ready to step out of your comfort zone and initiate change. You are ready to stand up, stand out, and become a leader, and now you know the tools that will help you use a structured approach.

Changing how you think about your employer and your boss is a crucial first step in making an impact. Think of your boss as your customer. You will feel valued and will make a difference sooner than you think.

"If your actions inspire others to dream more, learn more, do more and become more, you are a leader."

—John Quincy Adams

THE 10 COMMANDMENTS

Here are the 10 commandments of *Leading from Any Seat*:

1. Have the desire to change things around you for the better, the curiosity to question everything, and the courage to challenge the status quo.

2. Think of your manager and your peers as your customers and treat them accordingly. Listen to them and try to understand their needs as best as you can, using the **CTQ Tree** and the **Perspective Pie**.

3. Understand what you are working on from the start. Use the **Project Charter** to capture the problem you are trying to solve, the **Stakeholder Analysis** to ensure that you involve the right people, and the **RACI Matrix** to clarify the roles and responsibilities within the team.

4. Start high and get low. Start at a high level with the **SIPOC** to see the full picture, and get into more details using the **Process Flow Diagram**. Keep an eye out for the **Eight Wastes** and eliminate them.

5. Go beyond symptoms and get to the root cause of a problem. Brainstorm with the **Fishbone** and drill deeper with the **Five Whys Analysis**.

6. Eliminate distractions around you using the **5S System** and the **C&E Matrix** to prioritize and focus on what matters most to your customers.

7. Be proactive; don't wait for something to go wrong. Use the **FMEA** to identify potential gaps and make sure that you have strong controls in place to prevent them.

8. Show results by leading the implementation of your improvements. Use the **Gantt Chart** to help you schedule and keep track of all the tasks. The tips in Chapter 8 will help you improve your project management skills.

9. Ensure that the improvements you implemented will stay in place by creating a solid **Control Plan**—and don't forget to review it with the process owner.

10. Captivate your audience when presenting your accomplishments and ensure that your emails don't end up in the trash by using the suggestions in Chapter 9 and Chapter 10.

Keep in mind that the tools you have learned from this book are meant to help you, not to create additional work. Use them only as needed. My hope is that this book will inspire you to take initiative and approach problems in a structured way instead of letting them overwhelm you.

If this book helped you have "aha" moments in your job, I would love to hear about them. If you agree or disagree with my approach I would love to hear that, too. Don't hesitate to reach out.

LinkedIn: ***www.linkedin.com/in/andreianca***

Email: ***aanca@msn.com***

FREE TEMPLATES

Download your free tool templates:

LeadFromAnySeat.com